D0753547

MASTER RICHARD'S BESTIARY OF LOVE
AND RESPONSE

MASTER RICHARD'S
BESTIARY OF LOVE
AND *RESPONSE*

TRANSLATED BY JEANETTE BEER

ENGRAVINGS BY BARRY MOSER

UNIVERSITY OF CALIFORNIA PRESS

BERKELEY · LOS ANGELES · LONDON

University of California Press
Berkeley and Los Angeles, California

University of California Press, Ltd.
London, England

Library of Congress Cataloging in Publication Data

Richard, de Fournival, fl. 1246–1260.
    Master Richard's Love bestiary and response.
    Translation of: *Le bestiaire d'amour.*
    Bibliography: p.
    1. Bestiaries.   2. Love.   I. Title.
PQ1461.F64B413   1984   844'.1   83-18117
ISBN 0-520-05238-2

Printed in the United States of America

1   2   3   4   5   6   7   8   9   0

This book is dedicated to the memory of
Master Richard
and to the memory of
his unknown lady.

PREFACE

"All men naturally desire knowledge."

Richard de Fournival used the opening sentence of Aristotle's *Meta-physics* as his introduction to *le Bestiaire d'amour*.[1] What had originally been the basic premise in a discussion of the science of wisdom now served to justify the amalgamation of an *ars amandi* with a bestiary. The idea was revolutionary. It is true that lyric poetry had occasionally used animal similes,[2] that the satirical implications of *le Roman de Renart* had extended beyond the animal kingdom, and that *le Roman de la Rose* had popularized love allegory; however, an assembling of the traditions had never been considered. Inevitably, the resulting product was not a mere sum of its parts. Instead, the improbable format of animal exempla allowed Richard to produce one of the most cynical and misogynistic analyses of love that had yet appeared in any European vernacular. The heirs of the new tradition—the prose moralists—would extend beyond the Middle Ages through La Bruyère and Voltaire to the present day.

The bestiary tradition preceding le Bestiaire d'amour

Bestiary material was already centuries old when *le Bestiaire d'amour* appeared in the middle of the thirteenth century. Early sources were anonymous: the motley fund of animal anecdotes which existed in

Eastern Mediterranean folk literature, preserved and perpetuated endlessly by oral tradition. Eventually some stories were written down in a more permanent form by such compilers as Bolos of Mendes (third or fourth century B.C.), Herodotus (484?–425? B.C.), Ctesias (whose *De rebus indicis* was composed around the end of the fourth century B.C.), Aristotle (384–322 B.C.), Ovid (43 B.C.–A.D. 18), Plutarch (A.D. 46?–c. A.D. 120), and Aelian (second century A.D.).

The most influential compilation for the Middle Ages was, however, the *Physiologus* (i.e., "The Naturalist"),[3] which was written in Greek around the second century A.D. near Alexandria.[4] This pseudoscientific work contained much material that was identical with, and probably taken from, the compilers mentioned above. The facts and anecdotes about plants, animals, and precious stones were then given a didactic application: each particular property or "nature" was shown to have allegorical importance as the illustration of a higher truth. The creatures of Creation thus acquired a new significance in the early centuries of the Christian Church.

The Greek *Physiologus* was undoubtedly compiled by a Christian. Many authors have been suggested: Ambrose, Athanasius, Basil, Epiphanius, Jerome, John Chrysostom, and Peter of Alexandria. It was much used by several of the Church Fathers and was, moreover, translated into the various appropriate languages of the Greek Christian Church (Arabic, Armenian, Ethiopian, and Syriac).

But the most significant translations were into Latin, and their popularity was widespread. The first known reference to the Latin *Physiologus* was in A.D. 496 when it had the doubtful privilege of appearing on the first official Index of the Church of Rome.[5] The Gelasian interdict condemned it as apocryphal (Saint Ambrose having been cited as its alleged author) and heretical (presumably for Gnostic tendencies): "Liber Physiologus, qui ab haereticis conscriptus est, et beati Ambrosii nomine praesignatus, apocryphus."[6]

Latin versions of the *Physiologus* multiplied nevertheless, differing from one another as a result of many variables: dissimilar Greek originals, accretions of new or old material, reordering, excision, and metrical rehandling. The oldest versions have been classified by M. R. James[7] and later, in more detail, by Florence McCulloch[8] as follows:

1. Version Y.
2. Version A.
3. Version C.
4. Glossary of Ansileubus, known also as *Fragments alphabétiques*.
5. Version B.[9]

Of the above it was Version B that was most productive of new adaptations. These too have been grouped by Florence McCulloch into the following families:

1. Version B-Is.
   Version H (*De bestiis et aliis rebus* I and II, ed. *Patrologia Latina*, 177, where it is wrongly attributed to Hugh of St. Victor.)
2. The bestiary (*De bestiis et aliis rebus III*. For comments on the complete text, see F. J. Carmody, *Speculum* XIII (1938), 153–159.
3. Five thirteenth-century manuscripts:
   Camb., Fitzwilliam Museum 254, ff. 1–48. Early thirteenth century.
   Camb. Univ. Lib. Kk.4.25, ff. 48–86. Thirteenth century.
   Bodl. Douce 88 E, ff. 68–116v. Late thirteenth century.
   Bodl. e Museo 136, ff. 1–47. Thirteenth century.
   Westminster Abbey 22, 1–54. Thirteenth century.
4. One fifteenth-century manuscript:
   Camb. Univ. Lib. Gg.6.5, ff. 1–100.

Two versions that did not derive from Version B should be mentioned for their later importance. The eleventh-century *Dicta Chrysostomi*,[10] so called because of its *incipit* ("Incipiunt dicta Johannis Crisostomi de naturis bestiarum") omitted the lapidary elements, thereby becoming the first bestiary in the strictest sense of the word. This version also re-ordered the animal material according to logical categories. The "Chrysostom" version was influential upon some vernacular versions, for example, that of Pierre de Beauvais. It was also the basis for Gervaise's rhymed bestiary.

Theobaldus' metrical *Physiologus*[11] contains about three hundred lines describing twelve animals. The identity of Theobaldus has not been determined, but it has been suggested that he was an Italian Magister,[12] the abbot of Monte Cassino (1022–1035),[13] an archbishop of Paris,[14] and a canon of Rouen.[15]

The French bestiary tradition preceding le Bestiaire d'amour.

There was no reason that the bestiary material, in view of its universal interest, should remain restricted to the Latin-literate. In the twelfth and thirteenth centuries several French translations made the bestiary accessible to the wide audience it deserved. The earliest extant bestiary in the French vernacular was that of the Anglo-Norman poet Philippe de Thaun. He wrote it between 1121 and 1135, and dedicated it to Aelis of Louvain, queen of England. Philippe used the word *bestiaire* for his work, even though its contents ranged over beasts, birds, and stones. This broad use of the term was found also in several other early compilations. Philippe stated his source to be a "livre de grammaire" (i.e., a *Latin* book): "Philippes de Taün / En franceise raisun / At estrait Bestiaire, / Un livre de grammaire..."[16] Later in the work he identified his source more precisely as the *Physiologus*. His bestiary contains also some Isidorean material which he probably translated from an intermediary Latin version that had made borrowings from the *Etymologiae*. The scientific, theological, and literary contribution of Philippe's work is limited and, as its editor frankly says, "la valeur poétique du *Bestiaire* est minime."[17]

Guillaume le Normand's *Bestiaire divin*,[18] written early in the thirteenth century, also contained Isidorean interpolations. The religious significance of the material was elucidated with particular care, for Guillaume's prologue emphasized that he was providing these animal exempla to benefit the soul ("essamples por le preu a l'ame"). He did, however, add an occasional political or literary allusion, and his medium of rhyming octosyllabic couplets allowed him slightly more expansiveness and stylistic freedom than had Philippe's hexasyllabic straitjacket. The ordering of his material was essentially that of the B-Is Latin version, and Guillaume's primary purpose remained throughout the edification of the faithful.

Around the same time Gervaise made a French translation of a Latin version which he attributed to John Chrysostom (see above, p. xi): "Celui qui les bestes descrist / Et qui lor natures escrit / Fu Johanz Boche d'or nommez, / Crisothomus rest apelez").[19] The work was short (twelve hundred and eighty octosyllabic couplets) and, like the source it cited, omitted lapidary material from its contents.

Yet another bestiary appeared in or around the same decade, composed by Pierre de Beauvais (also known as Pierre le Picard).[20] This particular collection seems to have been structured first as thirty-eight chapters, which were then expanded with material from several sources beyond the *Physiologus*, and there are enough resemblances between the material of Pierre's long version and Richard de Fournival's *Bestiaire d'amour* to suggest that Richard had some familiarity with the work of his fellow countryman. Furthermore, Pierre pioneered the tradition of vernacular prose for the bestiary, explaining the reason in his prologue. A bishop patron had wished him to translate the *Physiologus* into French without rhyme, because rhyme necessitated the use of words extraneous to the truth—"rime se feit afaitier de mos concueillis hors de vérité."[21] In this respect at least Pierre renewed the bestiary tradition (unless, of course, one wishes to regard the introduction of prose as a contributing factor to its demise!).

Le Bestiaire d'amour.

Richard de Fournival was born at Amiens on October 10, 1201. He was the son of Roger de Fournival (a personal physician to King Philip Augustus) and of Elisabeth de la Pierre.[22] His half brother Arnoul, doctor of theology, was the bishop of Amiens from 1236 to 1246, and Richard was successively canon, deacon, and chancellor of the Chapter of Notre Dame in the same city. In addition, Richard had the ecclesiastical appointments of a canonric in Rouen and a chaplaincy to a cardinal, Robert de Sommercote. He was a licensed surgeon, by authority of Gregory IX, a privilege that was confirmed a second time in 1246 by Innocent IV.

His extraordinary erudition is demonstrated in his *Biblionomia*,[23] written around 1250, where he catalogued the contents of his library: the books he had inherited, acquired, or commissioned to be copied for his use. The *Biblionomia* introduced and described 162 manuscripts, principally philosophical, mathematical, astronomical, and medical, with a group of theological and legal texts at the end. After Richard's death in 1260 the library thus catalogued was transferred, through Gérard d'Abbeville, to the Collège de Sorbonne. Scholars continue to work upon the identification and reconstruction of the original collection.[24]

Contemporary researchers continue to work also on certain problems of authorship concerning Richard's own compositions. He is known to

have been the author of at least twenty-one lyric *chansons*,[25] preserved in fourteen manuscripts. There is also no question concerning his authorship of *le Bestiaire d'amour*, nor of its subsequent rhymed version[26] (although the motive for his attempt to convert the original version into rhyme is unclear, given his emphatic rejection of verse initially!). Certain technical treatises were also produced: the *Biblionomia* (see above), *Nativitas*,[27] and *De arte alchemica*.[28] It is probable that he wrote also *Commens d'amours*,[29] *Consaus d'amours*,[30] *Puissance d'amours*,[31] and *De Vetula*,[32] and he has been suggested as the author of *Amistié de vraie amour*,[33] *Hec sunt duodecim signa*,[34] and *Dis des quatre sereurs*.[35]

It is clear from the prologue to *le Bestiaire d'amour* that Richard singled that work out from the above titles as an achievement of particular artistic merit which contributed to the common stock of human knowledge. Not all modern critics share his view and, while this is not in itself surprising—authors and critics often differ over performance— critical opinion in this case seems singularly uninformed at times. Some literary historians (Lanson, Tuffrau, and Brereton)[36] have overlooked it. Paul Meyer's neglect of it is more calculated: "l'auteur s'ingénie à retrouver dans les propriétés des animaux les sentiments variés d'un amant pour sa dame. C'est un badinage littéraire qui nous semble froid et monotone, qui toutefois a été apprécié, car on en possède au moins douze copies. *Nous n'insisterons pas davantage sur cette composition.*"[37] U. T. Holmes has labeled it surprisingly as "an allegorical poem written first in prose."[38] And Piaget expressed dislike for it by opting for the "naive sincerity" of Philippe de Thaun.[39]

Its first modern editor must be held responsible for much of this lack of appreciation. Hippeau's text is unsatisfactory (and is hardly "enrichi," as it claims, by its forty-eight illustrations!), it lacks critical apparatus, and the editor in his prefatory comments virtually apologizes for releasing upon the world what he calls "fadeurs," "ces fleurs de l'histoire naturelle rassemblées en bouquets à Chloris."[40]

Richard's intentions, however, were neither trite nor insignificant. The juxtaposition of the two traditions, bestiary literature and love literature, could not produce two parallel sets of *lieux communs*. Instead, the shock of the two irreconcilables necessarily jarred both, forcing a reexamination of all the accepted truths by misusing them. Moreover, for

this iconoclastic bestiary Richard vehemently rejected the medium of poetry, thus allying himself with the growing tendency among French vernacular writers to use prose for serious didacticism. That his bitter destructiveness could be assessed by his editor as sentimental "fadeurs" is the ultimate irony!

From the beginning Richard's love bestiary was a challenge to the Platonic idealism of contemporary love literature. Its title was already suggestive by its juxtaposition—the love activities of a man and woman were by implication assimilable (and often inferior) to the properties of so-called lower animals. "One may learn the nature of one animal from the nature of another." Richard's opening quotation also placed the work under the aegis of Aristotelian naturalism, and Aristotelianism was visible throughout in his themes. He began with memory. Less interested than Aristotle in the differences that memory creates in the animal kingdom ("Φύσει μὲν οὖν αἴσθησιν ἔχοντα γίγνεται τὰ ζῷα ἐκ δὲ ταύτης τοῖς μὲν αὐτῶν οὐκ ἐγγίγνεται μνήμη τοῖς δ' ἐγγίγνεται," *Metaphysics* I, 1), Richard concentrated on man's faculty of memory and on the main sources of sensory information, sight and hearing. By an extension of the meaning of memory, he then dedicated his work to the lady's memory where he hoped to live forever. That conventional dedication was immediately followed by a denial of her ultimate importance for, regardless of her favor, the intrinsic merit of his bestiary gave it universality. "For even if you did not love me, these are things which the eye must take delight in seeing, the ear in hearing, and the Memory in remembering" (p. 2). *Master Richard's Bestiary of Love* was therefore dedicated above all to Memory, in its widest sense of humanity's collective treasury of intellectual gains.

The five senses provided a thematic continuity for the heraldic series of bestiary exempla caricaturing the postures of love. Indeed on one occasion (pages 11–14) Richard's interest in this Aristotelian material almost diverted him from the "love" aspect of his love bestiary. In a long digression Richard expatiated upon the five senses, the four elements, and the compensatory activities of certain senses to repair the defects of others. He then acknowledged the structural lapse, which he would surely have regarded as embellishment, and returned from his disquisition on the power of voice with a repetition of the sentiment that had

precipitated it ("Was it any wonder that I was captured by the power of your voice?").

Another literary convention, that of lyric poetry, authorized Richard's direct personal address of an unnamed "belle dame sans merci." The practice had a certain convenience which the twentieth-century reader, educated in the personal outpourings that have resulted from Romanticism, might overlook. In the Middle Ages the lover-narrator's seemingly personal "je" was in fact the most impersonal of conventions. Identity and personal characteristics of lover and lady were never readily identifiable by these means. Thus there was anonymity, if not universality, in the love conventions of the age, and Richard's "fair, sweetest love" need not have been one particular female in his immediate surroundings. She could just as well have been a composite fiction by which he attacked a whole convention.

Challenge is an obvious component in the image by which Richard described his work. *Le Bestiaire d'amour* was his "arrière-ban" (p. 2), a metaphor that, like much love-lyric terminology, originated in the vocabulary of feudal warfare. It signified the king's total levy of all vassals to support an all-out war. The representation of love as war was far from new, but it acquired a new psychological profundity in *le Bestiaire d'amour*. Richard explicitly renounced the writing of love poetry for his most important work on love. Its serious intent was reinforced by the use of prose. This treatise would be true in a way that (by implication) his poetry was not. The nature of that truth deserves careful attention.

No great significance should be attached to the ostensible declarations of love, which contain the usual topoi of the lover's inexpressible, eternal passion, his inferiority to his lady, and the need for discretion. They are belied by the real message that is conveyed by Richard's deployment of bestiary imagery. His introductory animal, the cock, was an immediate surprise. Medieval bestiaries, whether Latin or French, had traditionally opened with the lion, king of all beasts, symbol of the Lion of Judah, whereas the cock was little used in traditional collections—it is found in only a few extant versions of the *Physiologus*. Moreover, Richard had prepared the way for the regal image by proclaiming *le Bestiaire d'amour* to be the "arrière-ban" of a king. His representation of himself as a cock was therefore anticlimactic. Its shock value may have been in-

creased even further for contemporaries by the traditional association of 'gallus" (cock, and also priest of Cybele) with castration: "Gallus a castratione vocatus; inter ceteras enim aves solo testiculi adimuntur. Veteres enim abscisos gallos vocabant," Isidore of Seville, *Etymologiae* XII, vii, 50. Richard's purpose was, however, to develop the prologue's theme of hearing by this first image which introduces five similes for himself as a futile, impotent, rejected poet. The continuation of the prologue's theme of hearing, door to memory, is also progressive toward an anticlimax. Richard, recognizing love's midnight of the soul, must like the cock be more forceful in his expression; desperate like the hungry ass he must put all his effort into braying; deprived of speech because like the wolf he has been perceived by the woman (here symbolized by the man—a not atypical masculinization!) he has decided not to emulate the cricket which wastes its life in song, or the swan whose best song is an indicator of portending death.

The series is brought to an abrupt end with an image of revulsion. Richard would like to recall his words as the dog re-eats its vomit. The brutality of this shock image shifts the allegory in the direction now of woman's love. The reasons that her reactions are usually incompatible with a man's are visible through the three natures of the wolf (now used, it will be noted, for a different purpose from its first). A woman is unable to love in any way but totally, she is inconsistent in that she manifests love only when a man is distant from her, and she punishes herself when she has been indiscreet enough to reveal the degree of her passion.

The manner in which Richard uses his animal imagery should by now be visible. When selecting his material his criterion has been its relevance to the aspects of love that he wishes to develop. He has not hesitated to reorder or to use the same animal again when a different quality becomes appropriate. He has been careful nevertheless to maintain a rigid plan of his own and to exclude picturesque details that are only marginally relevant. For example, when speaking of himself as being like the wild ass, he does *not* use its well-known habit of jealously emasculating all the rival males in the herd. That property was possibly pertinent later in the love bestiary as an expression at least of the lover's male desires—he does denigrate potential rivals later in the work—but for the moment it would damage the portrait of a futile impotent, singing foolishly to a dominant woman. Occasionally the didactic implications of his imagery *do* seem to verge upon contradiction, but this is not the willy-nilly collection of all possible exempla that had characterized the conventional bestiary. For example, the tripartite complexity of the wolf's nature is a realistic expression of the Ovidian truism that "sunt diuersa puellis / Pectora" (*Ars amatoria* I, 755).

The analysis of woman's love through the three natures of the wolf is obviously a descriptive use of the imported imagery. Like the traditional bestiary, *le Bestiaire d'amour* used its images prescriptively also. Richard has the nature of the cock, discriminating between the hours of darkness[41] and reacting appropriately (descriptive), but he urges the inadvisability of emulating the cricket, which therefore serves prescriptively as a warning. The didacticism is never spiritual, however, and there is no observable pattern in the preservation of good-bad symbolism. One might have expected, for example, that Christ imagery would now be used for the poet and Devil imagery for the rivals, but no such automatic equivalences can be made. Much unfavorable devil imagery has been assimilated to the analysis of woman's love, but she has also been equated with the panther, symbol of Jesus Christ, and the ostrich, neglecting earthly concerns.

A listing of the imagery used by Richard either descriptively, prescriptively, or, sometimes, both is as follows:

Woman or woman's love—wolf (3 natures), viper, crow, weasel, caladrius, siren, panther, swallow, weasel (2d time), lion, pelican, beaver, crocodile, female monkey, partridge, ostrich, screech owl (old mother), hoopoe (old mother), eagle, crocodile (2d time), elephant, dove.

Man or Man's love—cock, ass, wolf, cricket, swan, dog, asp, tiger, unicorn, crane, peacock, lion, chicken, woodpecker, baby monkey, baby partridge, ostrich egg, baby screech owl, baby hoopoe.

Love—crow, hunter, lion.

Love's *méchants*—swallows, hedgehog, hydra, viper, baby monkey, serra, dragon, whale, fox, vulture.[42]

The woman similes slightly outnumber the other categories. They are also different in kind, for they generally imply criticism of her behavior in love or suggest preferable models for her to follow. The male similes tend rather to recommend self-preservation while making assurances of selflessness and enduring devotion. Richard's most persistent advice to the woman is to be nurturing and consequently he assumes both explicitly and implicitly the role of her child. He twice addresses her directly as his mother (p. 30). She is the ostrich that abandons its egg in the sand. He wishes she resembled the male crow which nurtures its young as soon as it recognizes them by their plumage, or the male pelican which, when it has killed its babies, revives them with its own blood, or the male lion, which roars over its cubs on the third day to give them life. In an unusual version of the "carpe diem," "gather ye rosebuds" theme, he urges her to look to the future when he will look after her better than if she were an old hoopoe (traditionally associated with filthy nests!) or an old screech owl (fed by her children when incompetent and old).

Aggressiveness, nonmaternal behavior, and pride are the chief flaws he attacks in her love behavior, and for this didactic message he employs several male animal exempla or himself assumes a nurturing role (see above). The precedent for occasional masculinization of the female beloved was already to be found in Provençal love-poetry [43] with the lady's seigneurial title of "midons" ("my lord"). The lady's merciless pride was also a traditional topos of love literature. Richard's new development of the conventions with his suggestive animal exempla revealed the ambivalence and the misogyny of the tradition as much as Richard's personal reactions to it. The basic content was not, after all, altered when animal imagery supplanted classical Cupids and Venuses. Love remained tyrannical and arbitrary. Love was now a crow picking out a man's brain through his eye sockets (cf. arrows piercing his eyes). The more intelligent his brain, the better the prey. Love's colors were now appropriately the black feathers of baby crows. Love was death; love was a wound leaving irremediable scars; love was *impedimenta*, trappings, clothing, which removed man from pristine purity and caught him; love was a pair of shoes which a stupid monkey imitatively put on and trapped itself. Love was overall a zoo of warring natures of which some were more dominant than others (e.g., wolf, viper, and crow). Furthermore, not all natures that deserved to triumph in love were able to reach dominance (see particularly the male similes).

Richard's adoration for the desired object was thus ambivalent, and it clearly included some resentment at the power women acquired through love. Woman's dominant emotion throughout would appear to be pride. The qualities to be sought by her should be humility, mercy, repentance, and discretion, none of which she apparently possessed but which (except for the last!) Richard apparently possessed in the highest degree. Although never explicit, for *Master Richard's Bestiary of Love* was not a religious treatise, an influential model must inevitably have been the Virgin Mary, the prime nurturer who eliminated rather than inspired insecurity. Her consistent humility, despite the ultimate favor, showed that she remained cognizant of her female unworthiness. It was hardly surprising that for Richard no woman matched this patristic model for womanhood and that he saw love as threatening, vicious, and even bestial. His prologue revealed the true *desiderandum*, and the justification for this iconoclastic bestiary, namely, wisdom. And it was certainly not by his re-presentation of ancient pseudoscience alone that he assessed his contribution to wisdom. It was by his conjunction of that material with his own analysis of love.

The style in which Richard wrote his bestiary is not, however, iconoclastic. Indeed, its archaizing didacticism still prevents some critics from perceiving its parody. Its exposition has all the repetitiveness (e.g., "the above-said nature," "this latter nature"), the sequiturs which are really non sequiturs ("wherefore I say unto you"), and the affirmation after negation ("It is not . . . rather it is . . .") of a sermon. Like a sermon also it is deceptively discursive, simple, and unmannered, with polysyndeton as a characteristic feature. Religious terminology is frequently used in a profane context ("repentance," "prayer," "mercy," "sins," "virtues of the soul"), although, as mentioned previously, the underlying didactic intent could possibly be religious despite—or because of—the parody. Underlying acrimony is occasionally apparent, as when Richard's prayers to his lady are equated with dog's vomit that has flown out through his teeth. But the general mood is that of bland irony. Even his apostrophe of his harsh, despotic lady (who would appear to be the embodiment of the castrating bitch so feared by contemporary Richards) employs two constants: "sweet" and "gentle." The euphemism matches classical Greek placating of the Furies with the appellation, "gracious goddesses" (*Eumenides*).

This is an understated, courtly style, for Richard obviously allies himself with courtesy, witness his comment that repentance is a courtly sort of vengeance. He is not devoid of courtly preciousness either. His interior monologues, ironic exclamations, rhetorical questions, and apostrophizing are reminiscent of a Chrétien de Troyes. Rhetoric is in fact everywhere apparent—in his abstraction, alliteration, antithesis, and the gamut of word-playing tricks. There are multiple Latinisms (among which his use of "desire" in its classical sense of *lack* deserves to be singled out as, I believe, unique in its time). And, of course, "examples" "confirm" one another in sequence. If this string of "confirmations" disguises secret laughter at his chosen bestiary medium, Richard generally manages to maintain his paradoxes in a manner that continues to puzzle the unwary. What is this *Bestiaire d'amour* but a "humble" cleric's love-bestiary to apostrophize sweetly an arrogant tyrant in a style of superficial courtesy cum patronizing didacticism? Quelles fadeurs!

A response to Master Richard's challenging arrière-ban is appended to the *Bestiaire d'amour* in a handful of manuscripts and, just as the identity of his "fair, sweetest beloved" was undisclosed in the *Bestiaire*, so it remains in the *Response*. Certain conclusions are, however, inevitable from the internal evidence of the text:

Its author was a woman of exceptional ability who could reason with cogency and argue with style;

Her philosophical and theological background differed markedly from Master Richard's; and

Her feminist defense of woman may have been a personal response directed specifically against Richard de Fournival.

Richard's prologue had claimed that the *Love Bestiary* contributed to the sum of human knowledge. The *Response* questions that claim by attacking the irresponsibility of an author who would "say or do anything by which any man or woman may be damaged." While Richard addressed an audience that was courtly and learned, the *Response* argues his first aim should have been the edification of the ignorant. The *Re-*

sponse's own introduction is reminiscent of the prologue to *li Fet des Romains*, whose clerical translator opined that every man who has God-given reason and understanding must take pains not to fritter away his time or live like an animal "beste." The roles are, of course, reversed in the *Response*, as an unknown laywoman preaches to a well-known cleric.

Richard had presented young women as irrational in their attitudes to love: "However well it may be proved to her, she may still say, if it suits her, that she wants nothing to do with it." The *Response*'s reasoned presentation belies those words. Master Richard's conception of love is attacked with a logic that is impeccable: "Although the crow seizes man through his eyes . . . although Love captures man and woman through the eyes, it does not follow from that that the crow resembles Love. Say, rather, that one must with the eyes of the heart compare it to Hate."

Taking Master Richard's statement that no one can know everything, the author presumes to state that she knows something which he apparently does not, namely that woman was created out of superior substance to man, and with superior workmanship. Her expansion of the dual creation of woman has the conversational vividness of the *Jeu d'Adam* (with a different bias!) and was presumably intended to counter the naturalistic view of love which was everywhere apparent in the Aristotelian *Bestiary*.

Master Richard had begun with the simile of the cock. She accepts that image for him, but moves quickly through the rest of the similes, reusing them all to contrary effect. *She* is the one who needs the arrière-ban; she is the wild ass braying in need of help. The dog to *her* signifies foresight, and becomes a model for her emulation. Richard is *not* clothed with her love, since she never gave it to him, and so on through the series.

She corrects a zoological detail in his description of the crane: it clutches pebbles in its *foot*, not feet, because it sleeps on one leg. And throughout her sequence of counterstatements she addresses Master Richard constantly as "dear lord master" as a counter to his "dear, very sweet beloved." She takes care to explain the reason for the respectful title. God made man caretaker of all creatures, even woman. Her obedience is, therefore, ultimately to God. God is, in fact, invoked at frequent intervals, whereas Master Richard had mentioned him only twice—in the relatively neutral context of the prologue when he described God-given memory.

Here and elsewhere the feminism of the author is obvious, and she eliminates from Master Richard's imagery many suggestions that are unfavorable to women. It is he who, by his fair words and deception, resembles the siren and he is the vulture (an identification he had fought in his concluding sentences). All the love imagery of the *Bestiary* is now turned to new purpose. In the *Response* woman is characterized by vulnerability, man by tyranny, deceit, and aggression. The pride which Richard had criticized as woman's worst flaw is here her supreme defense in the preservation of her self-respect and dignity. Death, which was for Richard a symbol for the denial of his love, is for the author the granting of that same request, "for the person who loses honor is indeed dead."

Richard had used the reproductive imagery of conception, birth, and nurturing to elicit maternal behavior from the beloved. The *Response* uses reproductive imagery even more extensively, and the maternal reactions of the author cannot be faulted as she deplores the behavior of the partridge, which allows another female to rear its young "through some defect in itself." But she courageously rejects Richard's bribe of future nurture for herself as demeaning to a woman who has not reached that degree of need. There is rich complexity in the human emotions displayed in the *Response*, from the sympathetic analysis of a woman's plight after she has been abandoned to the blunt social realism of her recognition that women will avenge their own distress at the expense of other women's virtue.

The intellectualization of much of Richard's reproductive imagery is another unusual feature of the *Response*. For the author of that work her "eggs" are the good reasons for self-preservation which she has conceived while reading Master Richard's bestiary. She expresses the hope that she will not conceive any thought which might be harmful if it were brought to term, however. She reproaches Master Richard for the potentially damaging ideas he is sowing in the ignorant—his words are represented as a bodily assault ("your words have hands and feet"). She restores the sexual threat implicit in the unicorn imagery. It is now the unicorn and not the maiden in whose lap it sleeps that is dangerous. Sexual assault remains implicit in her continuation of the unicorn description. "It has a horn in the middle of its forehead which can penetrate all armor. There is nothing so trenchant to pierce a hard heart as fair speech." Both authors interpret "illness" from love's "wound" as an indication of the aggressiveness of the opposite sex, but the *Response* would appear to use reproductive imagery more appropriately for the purpose.

Differences in orientation between the *Bestiary* and the *Response* are not only sexual but also philosophical and theological. The author of the *Response* shows obvious distaste for the Aristotelian assumptions that had caused Master Richard to portray love by animal symbolism. She reflects all the Platonic idealism of the courtly literature preceding her, believing in true love, and claiming repeatedly that woman is a *noble* creation. She suggests that Master Richard's requests are inspired merely by animal need, which ignores her totality. "I would be contrary to your disposition and you to mine, and we would be in conflict both in habit and in will."

To support her assertions concerning woman's nobility, she outlines a unique version of the Dual Creation which combines feminism and heterodoxy. By her account, Adam was a murderer in that he killed the first woman whom God had created, justifying himself to his Creator by the assertion "she was nothing to me and therefore I could not love her."[44] Because of Adam's departure from God's original plan of creation, Adam was ultimately responsible for the downfall of the world. For "if that first woman had remained, Adam would never have yielded to the sin for which we are all in pain." As for the second woman, Eve, "whence we are all descended," she was a superior creation to man although placed under his guardianship. "We are created of nobler stuff than you were, fair master."

This particular interpretation of Genesis 2:23 as a second creation of woman was characterized as Jewish error in the Middle Ages.[45] Whether current disputes within the Church (for example, concerning "bigamous" clerics) may also have contributed to its pertinence at the time the *Response* was written remains unclear. There is no doubt, however, that the author's version of human creation did not spring *ex nihilo*, and her calm conviction of its veracity reveals the degree to which her religious, philosophical, and social presuppositions differed from those of the chancellor of Notre Dame. The *Response*'s strong defense of woman's personal identity and role further individualizes it as unorthodox in the eyes of the Church (then and now!).

At this point another question inevitably presents itself. Was the author's impassioned defense of woman personally motivated? Many of her criticisms appear to be directed against Richard specifically, and his name is finally transmogrified into Reynard. In addition, the description of Richard's abominable nurturing abilities is extraordinarily vehement ("pute escole," "filthy upbringing," is hardly polite usage!), so that one wonders whether her brutal satire of clerics and her realistic comments about women deceived by the corruptors, reflect personal bitterness. But the reader must expect no confirmation of this surmise, since the author warns that if she had been involved in a compromising situation, prudence would dictate dissembling, as the lion covers its tracks with its tail. Her final dictum is that when a person does not wish to do something, there will be multiple refusals. She begs for mercy—as had Richard.

Thus, it is for the reader to surmise about the sincerity of each, and the only information is in the text itself. Despite the ambiguities, the *Bestiary* and *Response* provide knowledge of a complex age, however. Master Richard's manifesto of love in bestiary terminology constitutes a statement whose implications are brutally anti-courtly, anti-platonic, and anti-woman. It was these implications which a contemporary woman felt compelled to protest and, whether her protest was personal or in the name of all women, she has given us a poignant glimpse of woman in a reactive mode in a century that remains relevant to our own.

TRANSLATOR'S NOTE:
In the rendering of the *Bestiaire d'amour* and its *Response* into English, my stylistic choices were, more than usually, dominated by the styles of the two original works. Master Richard's ponderously argued sentences needed, in my view, to be transposed intact wherever possible, if his parody of two respected literary traditions was to be visible. It was similarly important that the tension between the coolly argued ser-

monizing and the impassioned "multiple refusals" of the *Response* not be destroyed by inopportune popularisms or by truncated syntax. For that stylistic end the suggestive archaism of the King James Version several times proved invaluable, and to that now-endangered tradition I acknowledge a lasting literary debt.

1 *Li Bestiaires d'Amours di Maistre Richart de Fornival e li Response du Bestiaire,* ed. C. Segre (Milan-Naples, 1957).

2 "Domna, aissi com us anheus
   Non a forsa contr'ad un ors,
   Sui eu, si la vostra valors
   No.m val, plus frevols c'us rauzeus."

(Lady, as a lamb has no power against a bear, so am I, if your worthiness avails me not, more feeble than a reed.) Guiraut de Borneil, *Anthology of Troubadour Lyric Poetry,* ed. and trans. Alan R. Press (Austin, 1971), pp. 12–13.

   "Tartarassa ni voutor
   No sent tan leu carn puden
   Quom clerc e prezicador
   Senton ont es lo manen."

(Neither buzzard nor vulture smells stinking flesh so soon as clergy and preaching friars smell out where the rich man is.) Peire Cardenal, ibid., pp. 290–291.

Rigaud de Barbezieux (ed. C. Chabaneau and J. Anglade [Montpellier, 1919]) used similes involving the lion, elephant, bear, stag, and tiger. The nightingale, phoenix, and unicorn were introduced into the poetry of Thibaut de Champagne (ed. A. Wallensköld [Paris, 1925]). See also A. Thordstein, ed., *Le Bestiaire d'amour rimé* (Lund-Copenhagen, 1941), pp. xiv–xvii.

3 *Physiologus,* ed. F. Sbordone (Milan, 1936) and *Physiologus. The Very Ancient Book of Beasts, Plants, and Stones,* trans. F. J. Carmody (San Francisco, 1953). For other editions, see Bibliography.

4 Cf., however, Max Wellmann, "Der *Physiologus,* eine religionsgeschichtlich-naturwissenschaftliche Untersuchung," *Philologus,* Supplementband XXII, Heft I (1930): 1–116. Wellmann places its date of composition as late as the fourth century and posits Syria as its place of origin. Lauchert, however, believed the *Physiologus* was available to the Church Fathers as early as the first half of the second century A.D. (F. Lauchert, *Geschichte des Physiologus* [Strassburg, 1889], p. 68).

5 Lauchert, p. 89.

6 Although the text of the proscription, found in the *Decretum Gelasianum,* is generally considered to have been an authentic ecclesiastical proclamation, there have been other views about its date and origin; see F. L. Cross and E. A. Livingstone, eds., *The Oxford Dictionary of the Christian Church,* 2d ed. (London, 1974), p. 385.

7 M. R. James, *The Bestiary* (Oxford, 1928).

8 F. McCulloch, *Medieval Latin and French Bestiaries* (Chapel Hill, 1960).

9 Editions can be found in the bibliography.

10 *Dicta Chrysostomi, Münchener Texte*, Heft 8 B (Kommentar), (1916):13–52. The earliest manuscript of the *Dicta Chrysostomi* in existence is Harleianus 3093, dating from the late eleventh or early twelfth century.

11 *Theobaldi Physiologus*, ed. and trans. P. T. Eden (Leiden, 1972).

12 M. Manitius, *Geschichte der lateinischen Literatur des Mittelalters* (Munich, 1931), III: 731 ff.

13 J. G. Thierfelder, "Eine Handschrift des *Physiologus Theobaldi*," *Serapeum* XV–XVI (1862):229.

14 G. Heider, "*Physiologus* nach einer Handschrift des XI. Jahrhunderts," *Archiv für die Kunde österreichischer Geschichts-Quellen* V (1850):546.

15 L. Hermann, *Le Moyen Age* L–LI (1940–1941):30–43.

16 Philippe de Thaun, *Le Bestiaire*, ed. E. Walberg (Paris, 1900; repr. Geneva, 1970), lines 1–4.

17 Ibid., p. xxii.

18 Guillaume le Clerc, *Le Bestiaire*, ed. C. Hippeau (Caen, 1852; repr. Geneva, 1970).

19 Gervaise, *Le Bestiaire de Gervaise*, ed. P. Meyer, *Romania* I (1872):420 ff., lines 37–40.

20 Pierre de Beauvais, *Bestiaire en prose de Pierre le Picard*, ed. C. Cahier and A. Martin, *Mélanges d'archéologie, d'histoire et de littérature* II (1851):85–100, 106–232; III (1853):203–288; IV (1856):55–87. It should be noted that although the oldest *extant* manuscript is in the Picard dialect, that is not in itself positive proof of the author's background, which remains somewhat mysterious.

21 The bishop here appears to be quoting almost verbatim from another patron of translation in prose, Count Renaud de Boulogne, who is cited in the prologue of one of the Pseudo-Turpin translations as having ordered prose "por ce que rime se volt afeitier de moz conqueilliz hors de l'estoire." See B. Woledge and H. P. Clive, *Répertoire des plus anciens textes en prose française*, pp. 29 and 100.

22 For the different vernacular translations of this name, see *L'Oeuvre lyrique de Richard de Fournival*, ed. Y. Lepage (Ottawa, 1981), p. 9 n. 3.

23 Richard de Fournival, *Biblionomia*, ed. L. Delisle, *Cabinet des manuscrits de la Bibliothèque Nationale* (Paris, 1874), II:518–535. Also, ed. H. J. de Vleeschauwer, *Mousaion* LXII (1965).

24 For example, A. Birkenmajer, "La bibliothèque de Richard de Fournival, poète et érudit français du début du XIIIe siècle et son sort ultérieur," *Etudes*

d'histoire des sciences et de la philosophie du moyen age, Studia copernica I (1970): 117–215. P. Glorieux, "Etudes sur la 'Biblionomia' de Richard de Fournival," *Recherches de théologie ancienne et médiévale* XXX (1963):205–231, and "La bibliothèque de Gérard d'Abbeville, *Recherches de théologie ancienne et médiévale* XXXVI (1969):48–83, and "Aux origines de la Sorbonne, I: Robert de Sorbon," *Etudes de philosophie médiévale* LIII (1966):82–83; 239–289, 294. R. H. Rouse, "The Early Library of the Sorbonne," *Scriptorium* XXI (1967):42–71, 227–251, and "Manuscripts Belonging to Richard de Fournival," *Revue d'histoire des textes* III (1973):253–269, and "A Text of Seneca's Tragedies in the Thirteenth Century," *Revue d'histoire des textes* I (1971):93–121. E. Seidler, "Die Medizin in der 'Biblionomia' des Richard de Fournival," *Sudhoffs Archiv* LI (1967):44–54. B. L. Ullman, "The Manuscripts of Propertius," *Classical Philology* VI (1911):282–310, and "Geometry in the Medieval Quadrivium," *Studi di Bibliografia e di Storia in onore di Tammaro de Marinis* IV (1964):263–285. H. J. de Vleeschauwer, "La 'Biblionomia' de Richard de Fournival du manuscrit 636 de la Sorbonne," *Mousaion* LXII (1965).

25 *L'Oeuvre lyrique de Richard de Fournival*. Also edited earlier by P. Zarifopol, *Kritischer Text der Lieder Richards de Fournival* (Halle, 1904).

26 A. Långfors, "Le Bestiaire d'amours en vers par Richard de Fournival," *Mémoires de la Société néophilologique de Helsingfors* VII (1924):291–317.

27 Unedited.

28 See A. Birkenmajer, *Etudes d'histoire et des sciences*, p. 119 n. 10.

29 A. Saly, "*Li Commens d'amours* de Richard de Fournival (?)," *TraLiLi* X/2 (1972):21–55.

30 W. M. McLeod, "The *Consaus d'amours* of Richard de Fournival," *Studies in Philology* XXXII/1 (1935):1–21; G. B. Speroni, "Il 'Consaus d'amours' di Richard de Fournival," *Medioevo romanzo* I/2 (1974):217–278.

31 G. B. Speroni, *La Poissance d'amours dello pseudo-Richard de Fournival* (Florence, 1975).

32 P. Klopsch, *Pseudo-Ovidius de Vetula, Untersuchungen und Text* (Leiden-Köln, 1967).

33 C. F. Pickford, "The *Roman de la rose* and a Treatise attributed to Richard de Fournival: two manuscripts in the John Rylands Library," *Bulletin of the John Rylands Library* XXXIV (1952):333–365; J. Thomas, "Un art d'aimer du XIIIe siècle: *l'Amistiés de vraie amour*," *Revue belge de philologie et d'histoire* XXXVI (1958):786–811.

34 Ibid., pp. 795–797.

35 Ed. A. Långfors, *Notices et extraits des manuscrits de la Bibliothèque Nationale* XL (1933):181–183, 212–248.

36 In their *Manuel illustré d'histoire de la littérature française*, and *A Short History of French Literature* respectively.

37 P. Meyer, "Les Bestiaires," *Histoire littéraire de la France* XXXIV (1914): 362–390.

38 U. T. Holmes, *History of Old French Literature* (New York, 1962), p. 240.

39 A. Piaget, *Histoire de la langue et de la littérature française*, ed. L. Petit de Juleville (Paris, 1896), II:172.

40 Richard de Fournival, *Le Bestiaire d'amour*, ed. C. Hippeau (Paris, 1860; repr. Geneva, 1978), p. iv.

41 This would be suggestive of the canonical hours if the recipient of Richard's prayers had not been profane woman.

42 Caution is necessary before embarking upon Freudian interpretation of these symbols. Psychoanalytic analysis, although perhaps legitimate, can be useful only after traditional connotations and, more significant even, Richard's explicit comments have been analyzed.

43 Love-lyrics, French and Old Provençal, are, with Ovid, the only specific references to sources in *Le Bestiaire d'amour*. For details of suggested influences, see C. Segre's edition, pages ix–xviii. Note also Richard's non-specific mention of "the ancients," "high philosophies," and his occasional use of a common proverb.

44. Cf. "God had created a wife for Adam before Eve, but he would not have her, because she had been made in his presence. Knowing all the details of her formation, he was repelled by her. But when he roused himself from his profound sleep, and saw Eve before him in all her surprising beauty and grace, he exclaimed, 'This is she who caused my heart to throb many a night!'" (L. Ginzberg, *The Legends of the Jews*, trans. H. Szold [Philadelphia, 1909], I:68).

45 "Cumque obdormisset, tulit dominus unam de costis eius, carnem scilicet et os, et aedificavit ministerio angelorum illam in mulierem, de carne carnem, de osse ossa faciens, et statuit eam ante Adam. Qui ait: Hoc nunc os ex ossibus meis et caro de carne mea. *Hoc adverbium "nunc" Judaeos traxit in errorem*, ut dicant aliam prius factam . . . et nunc secundam, quasi dicat Adam: Prior mulier facta est de limo terrae mecum, sed haec nunc de carne mea. Et Josephus dicit mulierem extra formatam in paradisum cum viro translatam" (Petrus Comestor, *Historia Scholastica*, ed. D. H. Vollmer [Berlin, 1925], I:17–18). The author's feminist expansion of the Creation narrative is not an impossible interpretation of Genesis 2:23. Conversely, it is not the only interpretation possible, as patristic literature has consistently demonstrated.

MASTER RICHARD'S

BESTIARY OF LOVE

LL MEN NATURALLY DESIRE knowledge. And inasmuch as no one has the capacity to know everything (although everything has the capacity to be known), it behooves everyone to know something, then what one man does not know another will. Thus everything is known in such a manner that it is not known by one man for himself, but rather it is known by all in common. But all men do not coexist together. Some die and others then are born. Our forebears knew what no one now alive could find out by his own intelligence, and it would not be known unless it were known from the ancients.

Wherefore God, who so loves man that He wants to provide for his every need, has given him a particular faculty of mind called Memory. This Memory has two doors: Sight and Hearing. And to each of these two doors a pathway leads, namely Depiction and Description. Depiction serves the eye and Description serves the ear. How one may repair to Memory's House through Depiction and Description is evident in that Memory, which guards the treasury of knowledge acquired by the mind of man by virtue of his intelligence, renders the past as if it were present.

This happens by Depiction and Description. For when one sees the depiction of a history of Troy or of some other place, one sees the deeds of those past heroes as if they were present.

And so it is with Description. When one hears a romance read, one hears the adventures as if one saw them in the present. And because one is converting past to present by these two things, namely Depiction and Description, it is clearly apparent that by these two things one can have access to Memory.

And I, from whose memory you cannot depart, fair, sweetest love, without the trace of the love I had for you being ever apparent so that I could not be completely cured of that love without at least a trace of its wound, however well I might contain myself, I should like to live forever in your memory, if that could be. Wherefore I send you these two things in one. For I send you in this composition both Depiction and Description so that when I am not in your presence this composition will by its picture and its word restore me to your present remembrance.

And I shall show you how this composition has Depiction and Description. That it describes in words is obvious, because all writing is performed to reveal the word and to be read. When it is read, the writing then reverts to word-form. It is obvious, besides, that it contains depiction, for no letter exists unless painted. Also, this composition is of such a nature as to need pictures, for animals and birds are naturally more recognizable when depicted than when described.

And this composition is, as it were, the arrière-ban of all I have sent you so far. As a king who goes to wage war outside his kingdom will take with him a group of his best men, leaving an even greater part behind to guard his territory, but when he sees the number he has taken cannot suffice for his needs, he summons all of those he left behind and makes his arrière-ban, so I must do. For if I have spoken and sent you many fine words and they have not served me as much as I needed, I must now assemble my resources in the arrière-ban of this last composition. I must speak as best I can to know if it might win your favor. For even if you did not love me, these are things which the eye must take much delight in seeing, the ear in hearing, and the memory in remembering.

And because this composition is my arrière-ban as well as the last hope I can muster, I must speak more forcefully in it than I did in all the others, as is said to be the nature of THE COCK. For the closer to twilight or to daybreak that the cock sings its night song, the more frequently it sings. The closer to midnight it sings, the more forcefully it sings and

the more it amplifies its voice. Twilight and daybreak, which have the nature of night and day mingled together, signify the love where one has neither complete confidence nor complete despair. Midnight signifies totally despairing love. Wherefore, since I have no earthly hope in the future of your goodwill, it is like midnight. When I did have hope, it was like twilight. Then I sang more frequently, but now I must sing louder.

The reason that the despairing man is louder of voice is found, I believe, in the beast that puts most effort into braying and which has the ugliest and most horrendous voice: THE WILD ASS. For its nature is

such that it never brays unless it is ravenously hungry and cannot find the wherewithal to satisfy itself. But then it puts such effort into braying that it bursts asunder.

Wherefore, it behooves me, when I find in you no mercy, to put greater effort than ever before *not* into loud song, but into loud and penetrating speech. I am bound to have lost my singing, and I shall tell you why.

The nature of THE WOLF is such that when a man sees it before it sees the man, the wolf then loses all its strength and courage. If the wolf sees the man first, the man then loses his voice so that he is speechless. This nature is found in the love of man and woman. For when love exists between them, if the man can perceive first, from the woman herself, that she loves him, and if he knows how to make her aware of it, from that moment she has lost the courage to refuse him. But because I could not hold back or refrain from telling you my heart before I knew anything of yours, you have escaped me. I have heard you say this on occasion. And since I was first to be observed, I am bound, in conformity with

 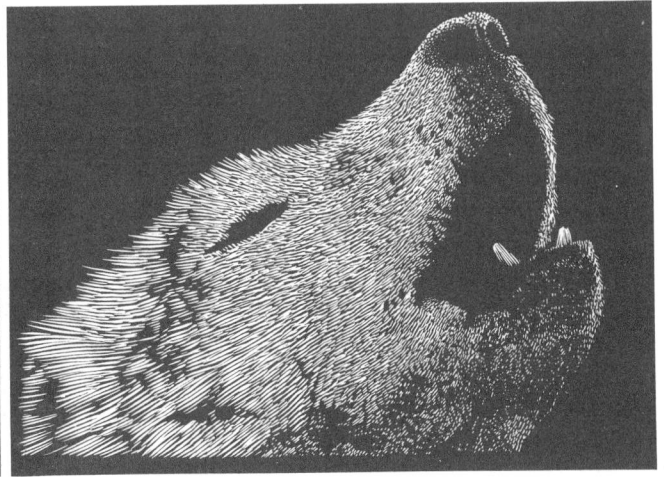

the nature of the wolf, to lose my voice as a result. That is one reason that this composition is not in lyric but in narrative form.

Yet another reason for the same is found in the nature of THE CRICKET, for which I have been much on my guard. Such is its nature that the poor creature so neglects to eat and search for food and it so delights in singing that it dies in song. And I took heed of that because singing has served me so little that to trust myself to song might mean even my self-destruction and song would never rescue me; more particularly, I discovered that at the hour when I sang my best and executed my best lyrics, things were at their worst for me, as with THE SWAN.

For there is a country where the swans sing so well and so easily that when a harp is played to them, they harmonize their song to it just like the tabor to the flute, particularly in their death year. So one says, when hearing a swan in full song: "That swan will die this year," just as one says also of a child who shows particular brilliance that he is not long for this world.

And so I tell you that because of my fear of the swan's death when I sang my best, and of the cricket's death when I sang most easily, I abandoned song to make this arrière-ban, and I sent it to you as a sort of counterstatement. For from the moment that the wolf saw me first, that is to

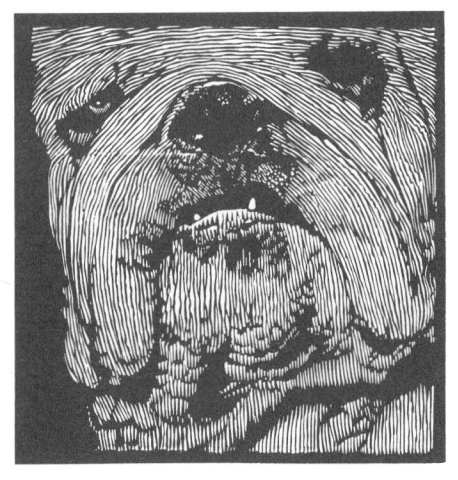

say, that I realized that I loved you before I knew what the fate of my love might be, I was destined to lose my voice. Alas! I have so often since repented that I entreated you and thus lost your sweet company. For if I could have acted like THE DOG, which is of such a nature that, after vomiting, it can return to its vomit and re-eat it, I would happily have swallowed down my pleading a hundred times, after it flew out through my teeth.

And do not marvel if I have compared the love of woman to the nature of THE WOLF. For the wolf has many other natures, also, by which there is much greater resemblance. One of its natures is that it has a neck so rigid that it cannot bend it without swiveling its whole body round. The second nature is that it will never capture prey near its lair, but only at a distance. And the third is that when it enters a sheepfold with the utmost stealth, it will take vengeance on its own foot and bite it very viciously if by chance some twiglet snaps beneath it and makes a noise.

All these three natures can be found in woman's love. For she cannot give herself in any way but totally. That conforms with the first nature. In conformity with the second, if it happens that she loves a man, she will love him with the utmost passion when he is far away from her, yet when he is nearby she will never show a visible sign of love. In conformity with the third nature, if she is so precipitate with her words that the man realizes she loves him, she knows how to use words to disguise and undo the fact that she has gone too far, just as the wolf will avenge itself on its foot with its mouth. For a woman is very desirous to know of another what she does not want known of her, and she knows how to protect herself securely against a man whom she believes to love her, like THE VIPER.

It is of such a nature that it is frightened and insecurely flees when it

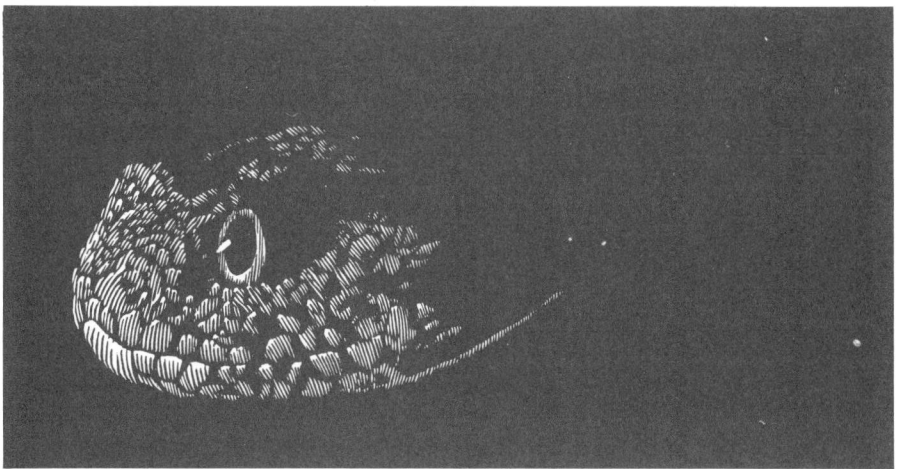

sees a naked man, yet it attacks him and has nothing but contempt for him if it sees him clothed. You have acted in exactly the same way with me, fair, sweetest love. For when I met you I found you to be of a gentle disposition and somewhat modest, as is fitting—as if you were a little fearful of me because of the newness of our acquaintance. Yet when you knew I loved you, you were as proud as you wished toward me, and you attacked me sometimes with your words. New acquaintance is like

6

the naked man, and confirmed love like the clothed man. For as man is born naked and then clothes himself when he is grown, so is he naked of love at the first encounter and exposed, so that he dares to speak his heart fully to the woman. But later, when he is in love, he is so enveloped that he cannot disengage himself. He covers himself completely so that he dares say nothing of his thoughts. Instead, he is in constant fear of blame. He is caught as surely as THE SHOD MONKEY.

For the nature of the monkey is such that it tries to imitate whatever it sees. So the clever hunters who want to capture it by ruse, spy out for themselves a place where the monkey can see them, and then they put

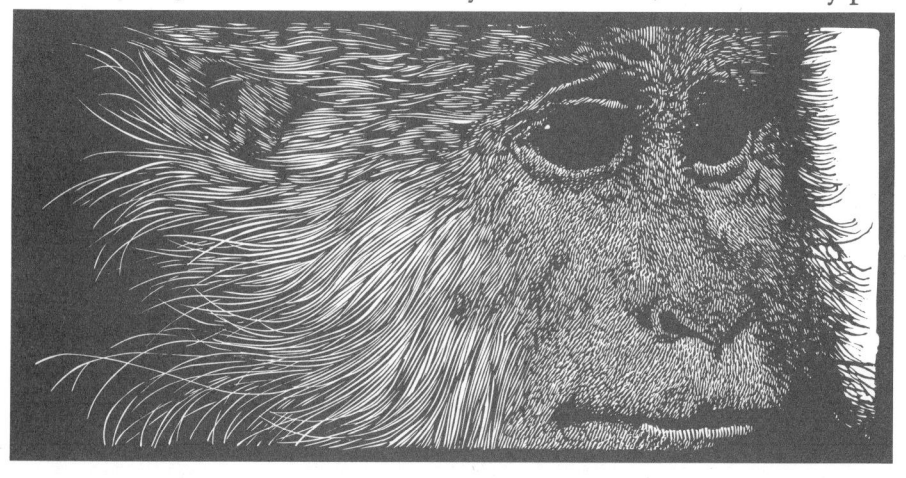

on and take off their shoes. After that they go away, leaving behind a pair of shoes to fit the monkey, and they hide themselves somewhere. The monkey comes and tries to copy them. It takes its shoes and puts them on to its misfortune, for before it can take off the shoes again, the hunter jumps out and attacks it. The monkey with its shoes on cannot run away or climb or scramble up a tree, so it is captured.

This example clearly confirms that the naked man is comparable to the man who does not love, and the clothed man to the lover. For as the monkey remains free as long as its feet are bare, and is not caught until it puts on shoes, so man is not imprisoned until he is in love. This example reinforces that of the viper, and by these two means I clearly see the reason that you were not as nice to me after you knew I loved you as you were before: the monkey is not captured until it is shod and the viper attacks the man when it sees him clothed.

Yet it seems to me that you should have done the opposite. I should have been better treated by you when you saw me clothed with your love than when I was naked of it. For such is the nature of THE CROW that, while its babies are unfledged, it will not look at them or feed them, because they are not black and they bear it no resemblance. They live on dew until they are covered with feathers and resemble their father.

This is what you should have done, I think, fair, sweetest love: when I was naked of your love you should not have cared about me, but when I was clothed with it and could carry an escutcheon of your arms, you should have cherished me and nurtured me in your love, however new and tender, as one hand-rears a baby. In love it would be better for the nature of the crow to triumph than that of the viper or the monkey.

For the crow has yet another nature which above all things resembles that of love. For its nature is such that when it finds a dead man, the

first thing it eats of him is the eyes, and from the eyes the crow extracts the brain. The more brain that it finds there, the more easily it extracts it. Love does likewise. For at the first encounters man is captured through his eyes, nor would Love ever have captured him if he had not looked at Love.

For Love acts like THE LION. If it happens that a man passes by and looks at the lion when it is eating its prey, the lion necessarily fears his face and glance, because the face of man bears as it were imprints of lordship inasmuch as it is made in the image and likeness of the Lord of Lords. But because the lion has natural boldness and feels shame at having fear, it attacks the man as soon as he looks at it. Yet the man could pass the lion a hundred times and the lion would not move as long as the man did not look at it. Wherefore I say that Love is like the lion, for Love attacks no man unless he looks at Love.

So Love seizes the man in those first encounters through his eyes, and through his eyes man loses his brain. Man's brain signifies intelligence. For as the spirit of life, which gives movement, resides in the heart, and as warmth, which gives nourishment, resides in the liver, so intelligence, which gives understanding, resides in the brain. And when man loves, no intelligence can avail him, rather he loses it altogether, and the more he has the more he loses. For the more intelligent the man the more Love strives in passion to hold him.

On account of this nature I say that Love resembles the crow, and this nature proves that its other previously mentioned nature deserves to prevail in love rather than the viper's or the monkey's, and that a woman should prefer to love the man who is clothed with her love rather than the man who is naked of it.

And I believe that some women do. But there are some women who have holes pierced in their heads so that whatever goes in one ear comes out of the other. Where they love they also refuse to give themselves, like THE WEASEL, which conceives through its ear and gives birth

through its mouth. Such women really act in that way, for when they have heard so many fair words that they feel bound to grant their love (and have thus conceived by ear, as it were), they then deliver themselves by mouth of a refusal, and out of habit jump readily to other words as if frightened of being captured, again just like the weasel which transports its litter to another place from the one where it has given birth for fear of losing them.

This last nature of the weasel represents one of love's greatest despairs, that one should refuse to speak of the very thing that is potentially of greatest value, and should want always to speak of something else. This despair conforms with the nature of THE CALADRIUS. When this

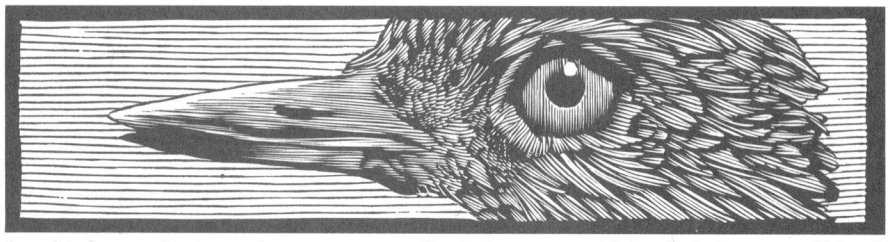

bird is brought into the presence of a sick person, if the caladrius will look that person full in the face, that is a sign that he will recover. But if the caladrius turns aside and refuses to look at him, the sick person is judged doomed to die.

And so it seems to me, fair, sweetest love, that since you are distressed I ever pleaded with you, and since you would readily have enjoyed my acquaintance and kept company with me provided that I said nothing of my sickness, you never wanted to look at me, a sick man, full in the face. Consequently, I must be given up for dead. For by this you have thrown me into the sort of distress that accompanies utter despair without hope of mercy. That is death by love. For as in death there is no recovery, so there is no hope of love's joy when there is no expectation of mercy. So I am dead, that is the truth. And who has killed me? I do not know. You or I, except that both of us are guilty, as with the man whom THE SIREN killed after she lulled him to sleep with her song.

There are three sorts of siren: two are half woman and half fish, and

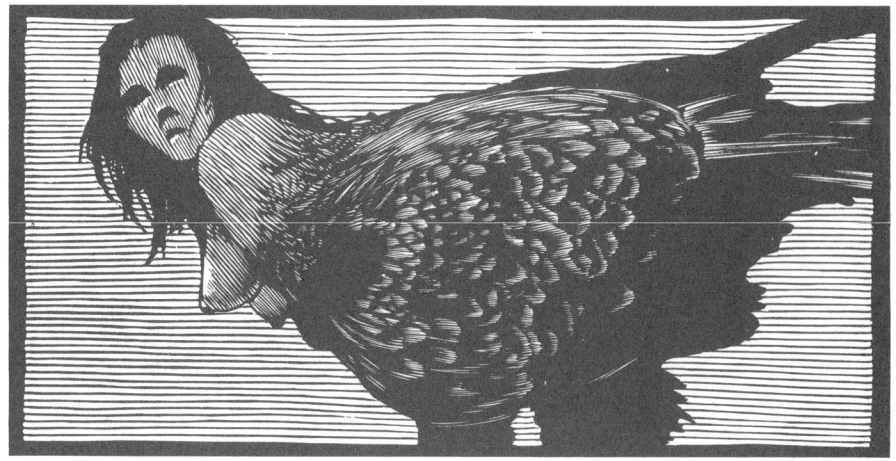

the third is half woman and half bird. All three make music; the first with trumpets, the second with harps, and the third with straight voices. Their melody is so pleasing that, however far away, no man hears them without being forced to approach. When he is near, he falls asleep, and when the siren finds him asleep, she kills him. And it seems to me that the siren has much guilt for her treacherous killing of him, but the man also has much guilt for trusting himself to her. And I am dead through such a killing, in which you and I are guilty. But I do not dare to accuse you of treachery, I shall take full blame upon myself, and shall say that I killed myself.

For although I was captivated by your voice when you first spoke to me, yet I need not have had a care if I had been as clever as the serpent that guards the balm. It is a serpent called THE ASP, and as long as it is

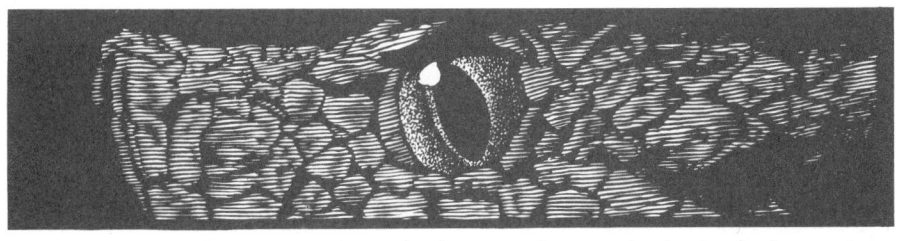

awake, no one dares to approach the tree from which the balm is dripping. When someone wants to get some balm, the asp must be put to sleep with harps and other instruments. But the asp is naturally so intelligent that when it hears them, it stops up one of its ears with its tail and rubs the other in the ground until it has filled it with mud. Deafened in this way, it has no fear of being put to sleep.

I should have done likewise. Nevertheless, I believe you knew very well how reluctantly I went to meet you that first time. And yet I did not know why this was, except that it was like a warning of the misfortune that has since befallen me. At all events I went and lulled myself with the siren's song, that is, with the sweetness of your acquaintance and of your fair words. When I heard them I was captured.

Was it surprising that I was captured? No, for Voice has so much power that it excuses many things that are unpleasant, as with THE BLACKBIRD. Although the blackbird is the ugliest bird in captivity and it sings only two months of the year, people keep it in preference to other birds because of the melody of its voice. And Voice has many other powers of which ordinary folk know nothing. One of its powers is that through voice Nature repairs one of the greatest defects that can occur in a living being. For living things experience sensation with five senses, namely sight, hearing, smell, taste, and touch. And when it happens that a living thing lacks one of these, Nature repairs her damage to the best of her ability by one of the other senses. Thus it happens that no man is as quick to see as a man who is naturally deaf; no man hears as distinctly as a blind man; and no man is as lecherous as the fetid man. For the nerves from the brain to the nostrils and the palate, along which the faculties of

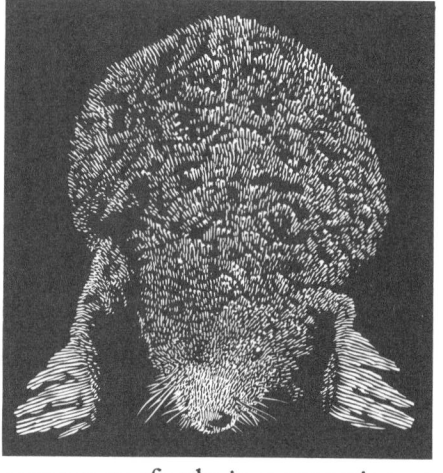

sensation pass, realize their functions more perfectly in proportion as they have less to do. And so it is with the other senses.

But among all the other senses none is as noble as sight. For none of the others brings knowledge of so many things, and it is repaired only by voice, as with THE MOLE, which cannot see at all, for its eyes are under its skin. However, its hearing is so acute that nothing, provided it emits some sound, can go unperceived and surprise the mole. So Nature repairs her defect through voice. For voice serves hearing, colors sight, odors smell, and flavors taste. But many things serve touch, for with it one feels hot, cold, moist, dry, rough, smooth, and many other things. And Nature thus restores the mole's defect through voice so perfectly that no living thing can hear as clearly: rather, the mole is one of the five animals which supersede all others with the five senses. Because for each sense there is an animal that supersedes all others, like the "line" (a little white worm which travels over walls) for sight, the mole for hearing, the vulture for smell (for it senses by smell a carcass that is three days' journey distant), the monkey for taste, and the spider for touch. And the mole has another peculiarity also: it is one of the four beasts which live on pure elements. Because there are four elements from which the world is made: fire, air, water, and earth. The mole lives on pure earth and eats nothing but pure earth, the herring pure water, the plover pure air, and the salamander (a white bird which is nourished by fire and whose feathers serve to make those materials that are cleansed by fire only) pure fire. The mole has these peculiarities, and in one of them the power of voice is demonstrated.

And it is not so surprising that voice can compensate for lack of sight by the sense it serves (namely, hearing), or likewise that it compensates for the defect of the very sense it serves. That is a power that is found in nothing else but voice. And it is written in the books on animal properties that BEES have no hearing. Nevertheless, whenever a hive of bees has

swarmed, they are led by whistle and by song. This is not because they hear it. It is clearly apparent by the mastery of their accomplishments that their nature is so noble and well ordered in their way that good and perfect order cannot pass them without being perceived by them. And those who have read and understood the high philosophies know well what the powers of music are. It is evident to them that in all things that exist there is no order as perfect or as exquisite as in song.

The order in song is so perfect and so powerful that it can move hearts and change wills. That is why the ancients had chants that were appropriate to be sung at weddings because no one who heard them could fail to be inspired to rejoice. They had others to be sung at services for the dead, which were so mournful that no one who heard them, however hardhearted, could hold back the tears. And others were so tempered and so balanced between two moods that they neither made hearts too light nor made them too heavy.

And since the order in song is so perfect, it cannot pass by the bees, whose structure is so orderly, without their sensing it. And yet they have not heard it, but they experience it through touch, which is the most general of the senses, and is properly served by several things, as has been said above. And so voice compensates for the lack of the very sense it serves, namely hearing, through another sense.

This power is one of the most miraculous that exists and no such power is found in anything but voice. And voice has many other powers by virtue both of speech and also of song, of which there is no place to speak now. May this much suffice you in accordance with our subject matter. And if voice has such great power, then it was not surprising that I was put to sleep by the power of voice. For this was not just any voice but was the voice of the loveliest creature that in my judgment I had ever seen.

Did sight help to capture me? Yes, I was more captured by my sight than THE TIGER in the mirror. For however great its rage if its cubs have

been stolen, if it comes upon a mirror it has to fasten its eyes upon it. And it so delights in gazing at the great beauty of its good form that it forgets to pursue the men who stole its cubs. It stands there as if captured. Wherefore clever hunters put the mirror there on purpose to rid themselves of the tiger.

Thus I say that if I was captured through hearing and through sight, it was not surprising if I lost my good sense and my memory in the process. For hearing and sight are the two doors of memory, as was said earlier, and they are two of man's noblest senses. For man has five senses: sight, hearing, smell, taste, and touch, as was said earlier.

I was captured also by smell, like THE UNICORN which falls asleep at the sweet smell of maidenhood. For such is its nature that no beast is so

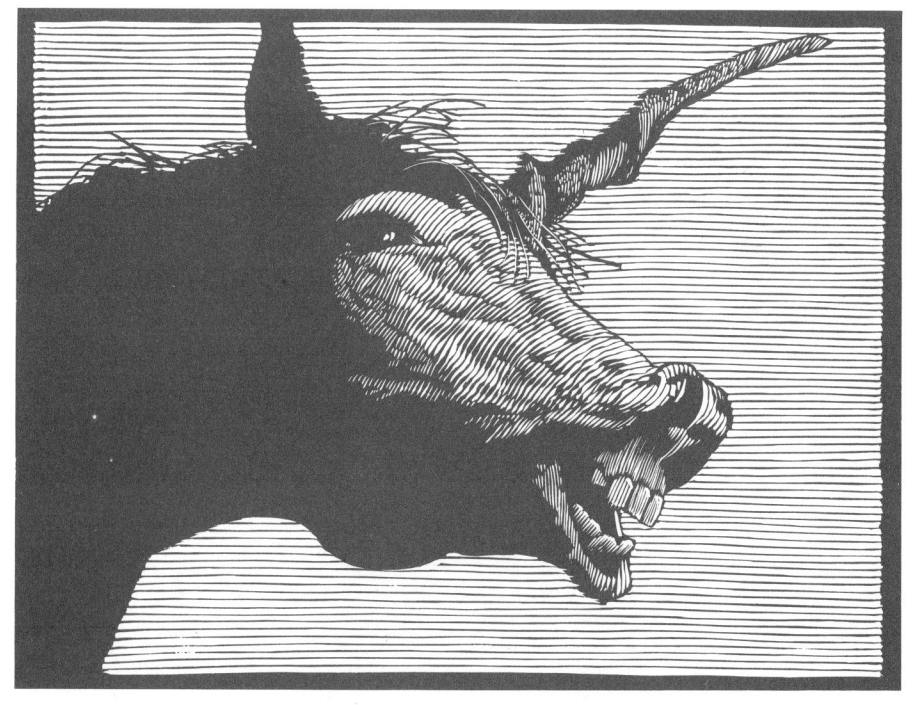

cruel to capture. It has a horn in the middle of its forehead which can penetrate all armor, so that no one dares to attack or ambush it except a young virgin. For when the unicorn senses a virgin by her smell, it kneels in front of her and gently humbles itself as if to be of service. Consequently, the clever hunters who know its nature place a maiden in its path, and it falls asleep in her lap. And then when it is asleep the hunters, who have not the courage to pursue it while awake, come out and kill it.

That is just how Love avenged itself on me. For I had been the haughtiest young man of my generation toward Love, and I thought I had never seen a woman that I would want for my own, a woman I would love as passionately as I had been told one loved. Then Love, who is a clever hunter, put a maiden in my path and I fell asleep at her sweetness and I died the sort of death that is appropriate to Love, namely despair without expectation of mercy. And so I say that I was captured by smell, and my lady has continued to hold me since by smell, and I have abandoned my own will in pursuit of hers, like the beasts that, after they have sensed the odor of THE PANTHER, will not abandon it. Rather they follow it to the death because of the sweet odor which emanates from it.

And so I say that I was captured by these three senses: hearing, sight, and smell. And if I had been completely captured by the other two senses —taste by kissing and touch by embracing—then I would truly have been put to sleep. For man is sleeping at the moment when he experiences none of his five senses. And from the sleep of love come all the perils. For death overtakes all sleepers, whether it is the unicorn who sleeps because of the maiden or the man who sleeps because of the siren.

But if I had wished to protect myself against this peril, I should have acted like THE CRANE which guards the flock. For when cranes group together, one of them is always watching while the others sleep, and each crane takes its turn to watch. And the crane that is on watch prevents itself from sleeping by clutching little pebbles in its feet so that it cannot stand firmly or sleep soundly. For cranes sleep standing, and when a crane cannot stand firmly, then it cannot sleep.

I say that I should have acted likewise. For the crane that guards the others is Foresight, which must guard all the other virtues of the mind, and the feet are the Will. For as one moves by one's feet, so the mind moves by the will from one thought to another, and man moves from one deed to another. The crane is putting stones in its feet to prevent its standing firmly and falling asleep when foresight is keeping the will so much in check that the other senses dare not trust themselves to it and consequently be surprised. The man who had taken these precautions would have had nothing to fear.

But the man who has no foresight is as damaged as THE PEACOCK is marred without its tail. The peacock's tail signifies foresight because a

tail, inasmuch as it is behind, signifies what is to come, and the fact that it is full of eyes signifies the foreseeing of the future. And so I say that the peacock's tail signifies foresight, and the term *foresight* means nothing other than to foresee the future.

That the tail signifies foresight is confirmed by one of the natures of THE LION. For the lion has such a nature that if when chased for capture it is unable to defend itself and has to flee, it will cover the tracks of its feet with the sweep of its tail so that no one will know where to follow it. A wise man who has foresight does likewise. When he must perform an action that would bring him blame if it were known, he makes provision as he does it that it will never be known, so that his foresight covers the tracks of his feet, that is to say the good or bad publicity that may result from his actions. Thus the tail signifies foresight and, more especially, the peacock's tail, because of the eyes that are upon it. Wherefore I say that, as a tailless peacock is an ugly object, the same impoverishment is seen in the improvident man.

Nevertheless, if I had as many eyes as the peacock has upon its tail, I could still have been lulled to sleep by the power of voice. For I have heard a story about a woman who possessed a magnificent cow. She loved it so much that she would not have wanted to lose it for anything, so she gave it to the care of a cowherd called AR G U S. This Argus had a

hundred eyes, and he never slept in more than two eyes at a time. His eyes rested continuously two by two, and all the other eyes kept guard and watched. Yet with all that the cow was lost. For a man who had grown fond of the cow sent over one of his sons who was marvelously skilled at making melody on a long, hollow reed he owned. The son was called Mercurius. Mercurius began to talk to Argus about this and that, and to play all the while on his reed, and he turned so around him, playing and talking, that Argus fell asleep in two eyes, then in two more, and so he fell asleep in his eyes pair by pair until he slept in all hundred of them. Then Mercurius cut off Argus' head, and led the cow away to his father.

And so I say that because Argus fell asleep through the power of voice, although he had as many eyes as are on the peacock's tail, which signifies foresight, it is not surprising if with all my foresight I too fell asleep through the power of voice, or that I died. For Death always stalks the man who has fallen asleep from love, as was said earlier of the man who sleeps because of the siren, and of the unicorn who sleeps because of the maiden, and here also of Argus.

So I am dead, that is true. Is there any remedy? I do not know. But what remedy for it *can* there be? The truth is that there may be some remedy, but I do not know what that remedy is any more than I know the remedy of THE SWALLOW. For it has been proven that when the swallow's babies are taken from it, blinded, and returned to the nest, they will not fail withal to see before they are fully grown. And it is thought that the swallow cures them, but it is not known by what medication. Exactly the same thing happens in the case of THE WEASEL, if its young are killed and handed back to it completely lifeless. The weasel by its nature knows a medicine by which it can resuscitate them. This is known to be absolutely true, but it is impossible to learn what the medicine is.

So I say of myself, fair, sweetest love, that I believe there is some medicine by which you can resuscitate me, but I do not know what the

medicine is except only that one may learn the nature of one animal from the nature of another. And it is well known that THE LION resuscitates its cub, and it is well known how. For the cub is born dead and on the third day its father roars over it and resuscitates it in this way. So it seems to me that if you wished to recall me to your love, that could well be the remedy to resuscitate me from the love-death which killed me.

So it is too with THE PELICAN. For it is well known that the pelican resuscitates its babies, and it is well known how. For the pelican is a bird which loves its babies wondrously. It loves them to the point that it will play with them very willingly. Now when they see their father play with them, they become confident enough to dare to play also, and they fly so much in front of his face that they strike his eyes with their wings. He is so proud of manner that he cannot bear anyone to harm him, so he becomes angry and kills them. And when he has killed them, he repents. Then he lifts his wing and pierces his side with his beak, and he sprinkles the babies he killed with the blood that he draws from his side. In this way he brings them back to life.

And so, fair, very sweet beloved, when I had newly met you and the newness of the acquaintance had made me as it were your chicken, you were so nice to me that I believed I might certainly dare to speak with you of what would please me most. And you esteemed me so little in comparison with you that my words displeased you. Thus you have killed me with the sort of death that pertains to Love. But if you were willing to open your sweet side so that you sprinkled me with your good will and gave me the fair, sweet, desired heart that lies within your side, you would have resuscitated me. The sovereign remedy to help me is to have your heart.

Now if it were for no other reason than that I have sometimes heard you say it annoyed you that I pleaded with you and that without that you willingly would keep company with me, you should give me your heart to be free of the annoyance of me, as THE BEAVER does. The beaver is an

animal which has a member that contains healing medicine, and it is hunted for that member. It flees as far as it can, but when it sees it can no longer get away, it fears it will be killed. Nevertheless, it has so much natural intelligence that it well knows it is being pursued only for that member, so it sets upon it with its teeth, tears it off and drops it in the middle of the path. When it is found, the beaver is allowed to escape, because it is hunted only for that.

So fair, very sweet beloved, if my pleading annoys you as much as you say, you might as well deliver yourself from it by giving up your heart, because I am pursuing you only for that. Why would I pursue you if not for that, when nothing else but that can be of any use to rescue me from death by love? Further, it is the sovereign remedy to help me, as has been said earlier. But it is locked up with a lock so strong that I would not be able to reach it, for its key is not in my possession, and you who have the key refuse to open it. Wherefore I do not know how this side may be opened, unless I had some of the herb by which THE WOOD-PECKER ejects the plug from its nest.

For its nature is such that when it finds a hollow tree with a small

opening, it will build its nest in the hollow. And to see the woodpecker's surprising feat people will stop up the opening with a plug which they ram in by force. When the woodpecker returns and finds its nest stopped up in such a way that its strength would not be adequate to the task, it conquers force by ruse and by intelligence. For it knows by its nature a herb that has loosening properties. It searches until it has found the herb, brings it back in its beak, and touches the plug with it. The plug jumps out immediately.

Wherefore I say, fair, sweetest love, that if I could have some of that herb, I would test whether I could open your sweet side to have your heart. But I do not know what herb it is, unless it be Reason. No, not Reason! Reason it is *not*. For there are only two sorts of Reason: the one is of words and the other is of things. It is not the reason of words. For al-though Reason has such power that one can prove by reason to a young girl that she should love, one cannot for all this prove that she *does* love. On the contrary, however well it may be proved to her, she may still say, if it suits her, that she wants nothing to do with it.

Nor is it the reason of things. For if one paid attention to Reason and Justice, the truth is that I am worth so little in comparison with you that I should have lost everything. Rather, I have greater need of mercy than of reason.

But on the other hand this herb is neither Mercy nor Pleading. For I have pleaded with you and cried for mercy so many times that, if this were bound to serve me, your side would have been open long ago. So I cannot learn what this thing is. So I cannot open that side. Yet there is no other medicine to reopen my life except to open your side so that I may have your heart. It is therefore evident that I am irrecoverably dead, it is true, so I must forget about recovery, it is true.

But, in faith, it is possible to find consolation of sorts in total desolation. How is that? If one has the hope of being avenged. And how could I be avenged in this? I do not know, unless she too loved somebody who did not care about her. Stop there! Now who would be so crazy that he did not care about her? No one, unless it were a type of person who has the nature of THE SWALLOW. The swallow is of such a nature that it never eats or drinks or feeds its young or does anything except in flight. And it fears no bird of prey, for no other bird captures it. And there is a type of person that does nothing except in flight. They even make love only in passing. As long as their love is in sight it has meaning for them, nothing more. Furthermore, they are captured by no bird of prey, for no love of woman or maiden exists which could hold them. They are the same to every female, like THE HEDGEHOG which can roll up in its

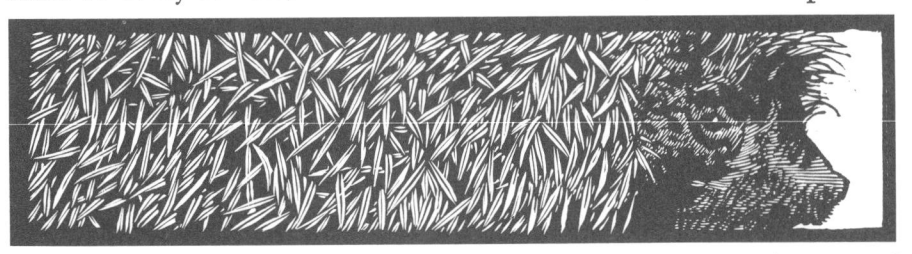

spines then one cannot touch it in any place without its pricking. And when it rolls itself in apples, it can load itself in every place because in every place it has spines. And so I say such men are like the hedgehog, for they can take from every place and cannot be taken in any place.

Wherefore I say that a man of this sort really could avenge me, but this vengeance would give more rage than relief to me. For I would prefer her dead and me dead than that she love another man than me after she refused me.

So what would I like? Rather that she did not love either me or anyone else. How then could I be avenged? I do not know, unless it were that she repented of the harm which she had done me. For Repentance is a courtly type of vengeance, and he is well avenged of his enemy who can lead him to repentance. So I would like her to repent after the fashion of THE CROCODILE. The crocodile is an aquatic serpent which common folk call a cockatrice. Its nature is such that when it finds a man it will devour him, and when it has devoured him it weeps daily for him all its life.

I would like things to happen thus to you on my account, fair, sweetest love, since I am the man you found, yes truly "found." For as one possesses without effort what one finds, so I am yours in that same sense that you have me for nothing. And since you have devoured me and killed me with love's death, I would like you to repent of that, if possible, and weep tears for me from your heart. In that way I could be avenged as I should like, for I would not want the other sort of vengeance at any price. Nevertheless I would fear that the other type of vengeance might supervene. For it seems an easy thing for a woman, when she repents of having let her loyal friend go, to bestow herself on another with less difficulty, if he begs her, as happens with THE CROCODILE and with another serpent called THE HYDRA. The hydra is a serpent that has several heads, and it is of such a nature that if someone cuts off one of its heads, then two more heads grow back. This serpent hates the crocodile with a natural hatred, and when it sees that the crocodile has eaten a man and is so repentant that it now no longer wants to eat another, it thinks in its heart that the crocodile is now easy to deceive because it no longer cares what it eats. So the hydra rolls itself in mud as if it were dead, and when the crocodile finds it, it devours the hydra and swallows it down whole. And when the hydra finds itself inside the crocodile's stomach, it tears the crocodile's entire bowel to pieces and emerges with great jubilance at its victory. Wherefore I say that after the vengeance of repent-

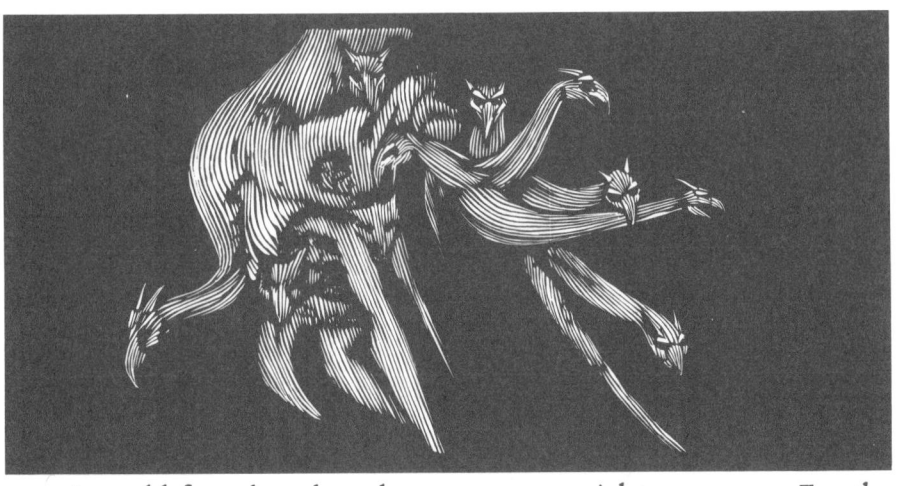

ance I would fear that the other vengeance might supervene. For the many-headed hydra signifies the man who has as many loves as he has acquaintances.

Stop there! What masterful authority and what a magnificent heart such men must have when they can break it up into so many pieces! For no one woman can possess it totally, but if each had even a fragment of a heart of such magnificence, they would then be completely happy! Nevertheless, I believe no woman gets any of him, rather he serves them all with his heart just like the player who holds the baton in the game of "brichouart"* and offers it all but leaves it with nobody. If he wished to be fair, he should at least leave it in one place. But since he wants to fool his companion totally, he carries it with him. That is how such men serve women and maidens with their hearts. And even if they left a part in every place, I should not think they could do any good by that, as one says of the man who, as jack of all trades, will be master of none.

But now I shall leave him and return to my subject. For I would wish that those men who make so many pieces out of their hearts should be dealt with so that their hearts shatter into pieces in their bellies once for all.

The other thing about the hydra is that when it has lost one of its heads, it gains several others, and it therefore gains from its loss. This signifies that if one woman tricks a man, he will trick seven women, or, if she tricks him once, he in turn will then trick seven times. I am very fearful of this hydra, and I would very much like my lady to beware of it, and specifically of those who show her most obeissance. For the man who will say most often, "Lady, help me to prove my worth," and who will say, "Lady, let me be your knight," is the very man of whom she should be most wary, if she wishes to keep her affair secret. For he will not believe he is her knight unless he gives her knightly service even while he laces up his leggings or is on his way to joust, in front of such a host of people that anyone of them may repeat it; nor will he believe that she has helped him prove his worth unless he has shouted her identity for all to hear while spurring on his horse. What is more—and what is worse—he seems to think that he must have a minstrel shouting from the parapets that his lord is performing each and every act of generosity and prowess solely for the love of that sweet creature whom the entire world must adore.

This is the type of man I would like my lady to be very wary of, for such men will treat her no better than THE VIPER treats the parents that engendered it. For the viper is of such a nature that it never comes into this world before killing its father and its mother. For the female conceives by mouth from the head of the male in this way: the male puts its head inside the female's jaws, she bites off its whole head with her teeth and swallows it and from this she conceives, and the male is dead. And when she comes to term, she gives birth through her side, and so must burst and die. Wherefore I say that I can truly call this manner of man a viper. For as the viper kills those who engendered it before it is even born, so these men cannot attain the worth of which they talk except by noising abroad the women who are helping them be worthy, who are *making* them worthy, if any worth there is!

I am very fearful of this viper, and I would very much like my lady to be wary of it. And I do not know who her viper is. But whoever he is, if my lady has received anyone, I would want the same for him and me as happens with THE FEMALE MONKEY and her two young babies. For the nature of the female monkey is such that she always has two babies in a litter, and although she has a mother's love for both the babies and she wants to nurse them both, she still loves one so passionately in comparison with the other, and she loves that other so little in comparison with the first, that one can truly say she loves the one and hates the other. So when she is hunted for capture, although she is unwilling as a mother to lose one or the other, still she tosses the one she hates onto her shoulders behind her—if he can cling to her, then let him and so be it—but she carries the baby she loves in her arms in front of her, and in this way flees on two feet. But when she has run so long that she is tired of going on two feet and must run on four, she must perforce relinquish the baby that

she loves and keep the baby that she hates. And this is not surprising, for the one she loves is not holding onto her, but she is holding it, and she is not holding the one she hates, but it is holding onto her. So it is quite just that when she has to save herself with her total body, hind- and fore-feet, she should lose the baby she is holding, and that the one that is holding onto her should remain.

I say, fair, sweetest love, that if you have welcomed any man into your heart who has the nature of the viper or the hydra or the hedgehog or the swallow, I would want what happens to the female monkey with her two babies to happen to you with him and me. For it seems to me that even if it were true that you love him more than me, you will still lose him, and I, whom you love less, nay whom you hate, would stay with you, because he is not holding onto you, but you are holding him, while I am holding onto you, and you are not holding me. *I say he is not holding onto you, but you are holding him.* As long as you want to do his will, he will love you, but when you want something that does not please him, he will leave you in a rage, as if he sought to pick a quarrel with you. So he is not holding onto you, he is following you at his own good pleasure, not yours, in the same way that THE SERRA follows the ship.

The serra is a sea-creature of wondrous size and with great and wondrous wings and feathers by which it projects itself over the sea more swiftly than an eagle flies after a crane. Its feathers are razor sharp. This serra I am telling you about so revels in its speed that when it sees a ship racing along, it races with the ship to test its speed. And it skims alongside the ship racing with its wings outspread for a full forty or one hundred leagues at a stretch. But when breath fails it, the serra is ashamed of being beaten. It does not give up gradually and do the best it can to try to overtake the ship. Instead, as soon as it has been outrun ever so little by the ship, it folds its wings and sinks completely to the bottom of the sea.

I tell you that he is following you in just this way as long as his breath holds out. For he would certainly do your will as long as it be not contrary to his own. But as soon as it were contrary to him he would not merely bear you a slight grudge to endure your will or to reconcile himself with you. Rather, he would abandon you completely on the occasion of one burst of anger. Wherefore I say that you are holding him, and he is not holding onto you. But although you are not holding me, it is quite obvious that I am holding onto you because, begging your pardon, you

have angered me so often that if for anger I had been going to leave you, I would certainly not have loved you as outrageously as I do. But I love you totally and I hold onto you so that if I had lost you without hope (as I have, I think, if one can lose what one never had), I would not betake myself elsewhere any more than THE TURTLEDOVE changes its mate.

The turtledove is of such a nature that when it has lost its mate, it refuses ever afterward to have another.

Wherefore I still have some hope, however faint, that since he does not hold onto you and I hold onto you, you are bound to lose him yet, and to keep me, in conformity with the nature of the female monkey. And I say emphatically that I hold onto you and would not leave you for another. For even if it happened that another woman who wanted me should behave toward me as one does toward a lover, she would not be able to deflect me from my love of you, as happens with THE PARTRIDGE. For when it has laid its eggs, another partridge comes and steals them from her, hatches them and rears the baby partridges until fully grown. But when fully grown so that they now can fly with the other birds, if they hear the call of their real mother, they will recognize her from the call, and will abandon their false mother who fed them, and will follow the other mother all the days of their lives.

Laying and rearing are to be compared with two things that are found in love: capturing and keeping. For as the egg is without life when it is laid, and does not live until it is hatched, so the man, when captured by love, is as if dead and he does not live until he is retained as lover.

Wherefore I say that, since you have laid (that is captured) me, there is no woman, if she were to hatch (that is, retain) me who would not lose me. There is no woman who could prevent me from recognizing I am yours forever and from following you all the days of my life.

Wherefore I say that since I would not abandon you for any other woman, and would abandon all other women for you, I am holding onto you, although you are not holding me. And it seems to me I am the monkey that you threw onto your shoulders behind you, the monkey that you cannot lose. Wherefore I still have some degree of hope, however slight, that I may remain with you in the end. But the waiting is much to be feared by my egg. For the egg which you have laid may well wait so long to be hatched that it will be forever sterile. For know of a truth that although I said that some other partridge steals the egg and hatches them, I shall not find someone to hatch this egg. Nor do I say this because I would like to find someone, but I say it because I have found someone who has said to me: "The woman who would invest her love in you would be a fool, and you are held in such true captivity elsewhere that she would lose whatever she might invest in you." And it so happens that this statement or its equivalent has been made to me by several— such women as would retain me gladly if they did not fear I was bound to abandon them at the voice of my real mother.

But since it is the case that neither you nor another wishes to hatch this egg, it may well be lost through long delay. And it would have been lost long since, had it not been for the modicum of solace which I get

from the restorative powers and jollity of heart which come naturally to me and from which I take comfort, as happens with the egg of THE OSTRICH which the bird leaves in the sand when it has laid it, and will never look at it again. But the sun, that universal source of warmth by which all things survive, nourishes it in the sand, and thus it comes to life, nor will it ever be hatched in any other way. So I say of myself who am the egg that is hatched by nobody, that I might easily be lost without a little jollity of heart that sustains me and is like the sun. For it is the universal comfort of which each man has his share according as God has given it to him.

But there is no warmth so natural as beneath a mother's wing, and no nourishment so good for a child as his own mother's milk. And if you wished to nourish me, fair, very sweet, beloved mother, I would be as good a son to you as the young SCREECH OWLS and THE HOOPOES are

to their mothers. For as much time as the screech owl spends in nourishing her young, so much do they for their part spend in nourishing their mother when they are mature, and similarly the young of the hoopoe. For when she is in poor plumage, she would never moult by herself as other birds do, but the young hoopoes come and pull out the old feathers with their beaks, and then they brood over her and nourish her until she is completely covered with new plumage. And they spend as much time brooding and nourishing her as she spent on them when she hatched them. Fair, very sweet mother, I would very gladly be as good a son to you. For if you wished to hatch and nourish me, that is to say retain me as your love, as it was stated above that laying was the capturing and hatching the retaining, know that there is nothing by which a faithful lover should test himself that I would not do for you.

But if you do not value my nurture as much as your own, and if it seems that I would not have rewarded you enough for your love if I had given you mine, I respond that there is nothing that is not equalized by love. For in love there is neither valley nor hill. Love is all one like a wave-less sea. Wherefore a Poitevin said that love that so undulates is worthless; wherefore also Ovid said that love and mastery cannot remain together on a single throne; and the Poitevin, who followed Ovid in this, said, "Pride cannot coexist with love." And that other who for his part said, "I cannot ascend if she does not descend" meant that, since she was higher and he lower, she must descend and he ascend to be one. The reason for this equality is to be found in the fact that the same path goes from St. Denis to Paris as from Paris to St. Denis.

And so I say that if you wanted us to love each other, it would be one and the same love from you to me and from me to you, and the one love and the other would both be of the same lineage. Wherefore the Poitevin said, "Unequal to you in rank, yet ranked equal through love." Wherefore I say that because it would all be one, I would bestow on you as much as you would have bestowed on me. For although at this time I am not as worthy as you, if you loved me, your love would improve me until I was worth as much as you, for it would raise me to your stature.

Wherefore it seems to me that I could be as good a son to you as the screech owls and the young hoopoes are to their mothers. But it seems to me that you have more than might be helpful to me of that pride that cannot coexist with love. You should cut it down or you could not savor the joy of love, as THE EAGLE, when its beak is so overgrown that it cannot eat, shatters its beak and then sharpens it anew on the hardest stone it can find.

The eagle's beak signifies the pride that stands in the way of love. The beak shatters when one so humbles oneself as to unlock the fortress that defends the tongue for the purpose of recognizing and granting favor. But there are some who unlock it in the wrong way. For they are consistently secretive when they should reveal themselves, and find solace by seeking out no matter whom to trust, and chattering lightly to him. I say that that is shattering one's beak in the wrong way.

They resemble THE CROCODILE. For all existing animals that eat in the right way move their lower jaw to chew, and keep the upper jaw

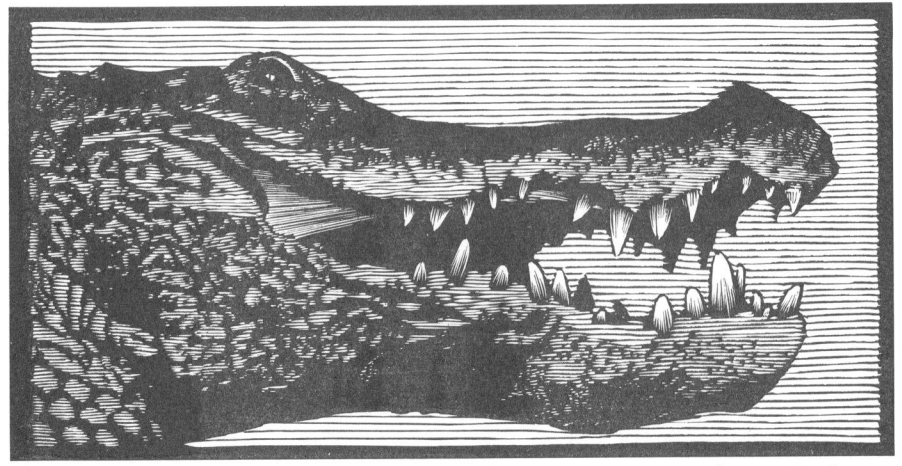

motionless. But the crocodile eats in the reverse way. It keeps its lower jaw motionless and moves the upper. So it is in speaking of one's love. For when speaking of it in a place where that love cannot be anything but hidden, one moves one's lower jaw. And who would hide love better than the lover? No one, for it is to his advantage. But when speaking of it to anyone else in the world, one moves one's upper jaw. The lower jaw, insofar as it is underneath, signifies what is concealed, and the upper jaw, inasmuch as it is above, signifies what is revealed.

Wherefore it seems that as the crocodile eats in a perverse way when it moves its upper jaw and leaves its lower jaw motionless, so a woman who speaks of her love to anyone except her lover, and is secretive with her lover, shatters her beak in the wrong way, because there are few people who are discriminating in the selection of those to whom they must talk. For a man may present himself as a model of fidelity, yet may bite treacherously and, on the other hand (and more frequently!), a man who has no intention of acting treacherously will not know how to be discreet about you, because it will not seem necessary for him to be discreet about you to another person when you are not discreet with him. Those men are like THE DRAGON. For the dragon does not bite anyone, but it poisons with a flick of its tongue, and some men do precisely that. They spread your news to someone else as easily as they heard it from you.

Anyone who wished to be wary of that dragon should behave like THE ELEPHANT. For the nature of the elephant is such that it fears no creature except the dragon. But between those two there is a natural hatred, so that when the female elephant reaches term, she goes into the

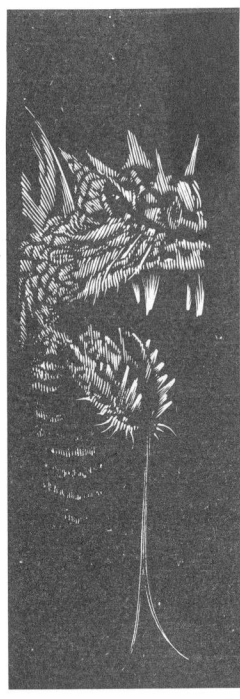

water of the Euphrates (which is a river of greater India) to give birth, because the dragon is of such an ardent nature that it cannot tolerate water, and if the dragon happened upon the young elephants, it would lick them and poison them. The male too watches by the water on the riverbank for fear of the dragon.

I say that anyone who acted in this way need have no care for the dragon. For giving birth signifies retaining in love. For it has been said above concerning the nature of the partridge that when a woman retains a man as her lover, she makes him her child. And anyone who gave birth like this in the water need have no care for the dragon, for water signifies foresight inasmuch as it has the nature of a mirror. Wherefore it happens that A DOVE sits very willingly on water because, if a goshawk approaches to capture it, the dove is alerted from afar by the shadow of the goshawk which it sees in the water, and it has time to flee to safety.

Wherefore I say that the person who acts with foresight so as to guard from afar against all those who have the power to harm is sitting well upon the water. Wherefore I say that water signifies foresight. Thus if she wishes to guard against the dragon, she must give birth in the water, which is to say that, if she wishes her love to be hidden, she must retain her lover with such providence that excessive delay does not drive him to such despair that he does mischief whence one can perceive his love while, on the other hand, she will not herself need to seek someone or other to provide her with solace, and to whom meanwhile she will joke about it.

Anyone who used such providence would not need to fear revelation. For one does not know in whom to trust, and if anyone wants to protect himself against the malicious, let him protect himself against everyone. For a man who is a treacherous renegade may give much assurance of his loyalty. The man who gives me most assurance of his word is the man I will trust the least. For when he takes such pains to be believed, he knows something that is to be feared and wants to exploit it.

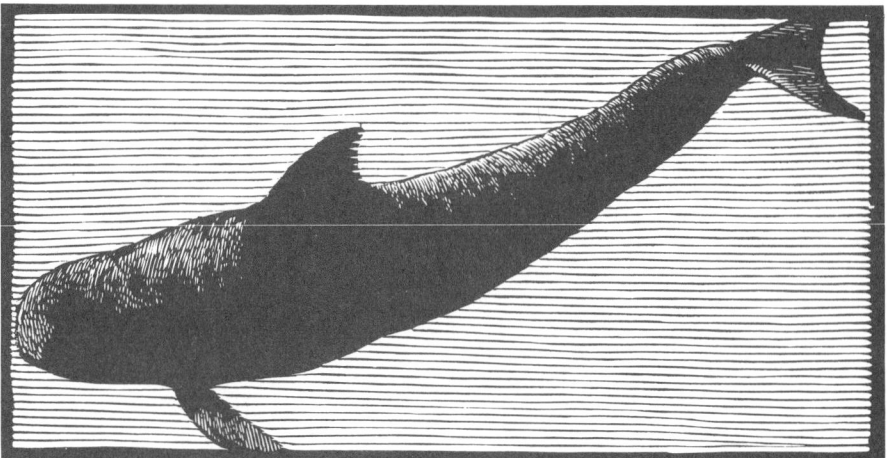

Many people are dead for having trusted in such guarantors, as happens with a sort of WHALE, which is so large that when it has its back above the water, the sailors who see it think it is an island, because its skin is just like sand. So the sailors come to land on it as if it were an island, lodge on it, and stay eight days or fifteen, and they look for food on the back of the whale. But when the whale feels the fire, it plunges itself and them into the depths of the sea. Wherefore I say that one must trust least whatever in the world appears most trustworthy. For this is what happens with most who become lovers. A man will say he is dying of love when he feels no pain or hurt, and these deceive good folk just as THE FOX deceives THE MAGPIES. For the fox is of such a nature that when it is hungry and finds nothing to eat, it will roll in the mud of red earth and will lie down with its jaws hanging open and its tongue out, as if it had bled to death. Then come the magpies, thinking it dead, and they try to eat the tongue. And the fox bares its teeth, seizes them by the head, and devours them.

And so I say that a man may act completely lovelorn when he does not care at all and is bent only on treachery. But perchance you will say the same of me. And to this I respond that one joins the army for many reasons. Some go for profit, others to do their lord's service, and yet others because they do not know where to go and are going to see the world. And there is a bird called THE VULTURE whose habit it is to follow the armies because it lives on corpses, and it knows by its nature that there will be dead men or slaughtered horses there. This vulture signi-

fies those who follow women and maidens to take advantage of them, however much the women may be hurt by this. And those who go into the army because they do not know where to go, and who are going to see the world signify men who love no one. But they cannot meet anyone without speaking of love, and they cannot speak of love without begging for it. They do not do this through treachery but out of habit. And those who go into the army because their lord needs their services signify the true lovers.

Concerning this I tell you that I do not follow you out of habit like a vulture. But I cannot by any power of words make you know the species to which I belong. But if you had kept me in your service, I would show you clearly by my actions that I follow you to do the service of my lady. Nevertheless, since no rational argument can avail me anything with you, I ask nothing from you but mercy.

Here ends Master Richard's Bestiary.

THE RESPONSE

TO MASTER RICHARD'S BESTIARY OF LOVE

Here begins the prologue of the Response to Master Richard's Bestiary:

A MAN WHO HAS INTELLIGENCE and discretion must not employ his time or his attention to say or do anything by which any man or any woman may be damaged, but the person who is able to say or do something which is profitable to the ignorant is accomplishing good work. So I have understood, fair lord, dear master, in your prologue, which you sent me in your request for love, and from which I find myself quite reassured. It has been most useful to me first to regard that prologue, which shows me that I cannot easily be wise about everything that could be useful to me. And truly you have shown me by rational argument that no one has the capacity to know everything, although everything has the capacity to be known. So it behooves me in the making of this response to employ great pains not to say or do anything by which a base-thinking man or woman might eventually ridicule me. For when you and I shall have done as much as we ought, avenging Love will render due reward to everyone.

Wherefore, fair master, I beg you in accordance with what you have told me, not to interpret it as villainy if I aid myself with your intelligence, according as I have retained some of it. For although I cannot know all that you know, yet I know something that you do not. Wherefore it is very useful for me to aid myself with that since my need is great, I who am a woman in conformity with Our Lord's good pleasure, Who did not want to make me of less good substance than He made you. And it pleases me to tell you how, although you have not made mention of this in your work.

God who by His dignity and power created the whole world and first made heaven and earth and all that is established in the one and in the other, afterward made man to be the noblest creature He could devise. And it pleased God to make man out of a substance that is not among the most suitable of substances. And from this substance, according to certain authorities, He formed such a woman as did not please the man whom He had previously made. Then it came to pass that when God had given life to the one and to the other, Adam killed his wife, and God asked him why he had done this. He replied, "She was nothing to me and therefore I could not love her." So Our Lord came then to Adam where he slept, and took one of his ribs, and from it fashioned Eve, whence we are all descended. Wherefore some maintain that if that first woman had remained, Adam would never have yielded to the sin for which we are all in pain. But for the very great love Adam had for the woman who was made from him, he loved her in the way that became apparent. For that love for her took precedence over the commandment of Our Lord, as you have heard on other occasion how they ate the fruit that had been forbidden them.

But I must abridge this matter and attend to what I began. So, since it is the case that Our Lord gave man mastery over every creature, even over the woman whom He had made of more suitable substance than man, Scripture puts forward a reasonable argument for why He did this. Nonetheless, He who was Lord of all formed man of whatever material was at hand. Then He took from man himself, as was said earlier, and made and fashioned from it WOMAN.

This is why I say that inasmuch as man had been fashioned by such a noble artisan, the substance was much improved after this process. So for this reason woman was made of equal if not better material than man. And in this regard let no one come forward to challenge the following truth: that if Our Lord's grace had not been so abundant as to cause Him to intend man to have dominion over every human creature we are created of nobler stuff than you were, fair master, but must nevertheless obey you by the command of our Sovereign. But God never did anything without reason, for it is fitting that this thing which derives from the other should be obeisant to it. Thus woman must obey man, and man the earth, and the earth God, for God was the Creator and Sovereign of its every creature. Wherefore everyone must know that he must obey that wherefrom he came, and principally Him Who made all, as has been said above.

For which reason, lord and master, I who am a woman must obey you who are a man, which is to say that I intend to put to use what seems good to me, and if there be anything else remaining, let it wait until it can be useful either to me or to another.

Since it is the case, fair lord, dear master, that you have proved to me by dint of reason that Memory has two doors, Sight and Hearing, it is assuredly very useful for me to know this truth. For since you give me to understand by this argument that memory is both treasure and guardian, I must certainly see to it and know that neither you nor any other say anything to me by which my memory might in anyway be impeded. For seemingly you give me to understand that I am all alone in your memory, whence you cannot depart, according to what you tell me in your composition.

Ah, true God, since it is the case that I am all alone in this treasure house, how useful it would be to me to proclaim this arrière-ban which you say is necessary to the king who cannot make do with the number of retainers he has taken with him! And it is apparent that the need is great. For I understand, in conformity with the nature of THE COCK, that you have spoken penetrating words to me, which are in your view necessary to accomplish your will. And because I am not wise enough to make use of what you tell me, I do not know where to turn for comfort, unless I give mind to THE WILD ASS of which I heard you speak. For you seem to be saying that it never brays before it is out of its mind with hunger.

In faith, I can certainly bray! For according to what you have told me, I have great need of help. For as you have told me concerning THE WOLF that its nature is such that, if man sees it before it sees man, it loses its strength and its courage, but that if the wolf sees the man first, the man becomes hoarse and loses as it were the power of speech, I must truly say that I was seen first by you whom I must for this reason call the wolf. For it is with difficulty that I can say anything to counter your words. Wherefore I can truly say that I was first seen by you, and I must thus be on my guard if I am prudent.

Wherefore, lord and master, I shall disregard THE CRICKET of which I heard you speak. For although it enjoys its song so much that it neglects to search for food and dies of starvation, *I* am not served by attending to your words, which appear to put me at your disposal. In my view, I must certainly not trust to them, in conformity with the nature of THE SWAN.

For you have told me that in the very year the swan must die it has the greatest desire to sing. Ah, God, why would I not be hesitant to do what could result in my misfortune, according to the nature of the cricket and the swan? By God, these two natures show me clearly that I must not be too precipitate to do something that would put me in a fool's power. No, I will not. Rather I shall be mindful of THE DOG whose nature, I have heard, is such that when it is in a place of abundant food, it takes what it needs, then garners the surplus and vomits it into a secret place. Then when famine threatens, the dog eats up the food again.

So must I do, fair lord and master. For truly I am bound to treasure the amount of honor I have, since you are so covetous to get it. But, in conformity with the nature of the dog, I must take care to keep for myself what good I can have. And if there is a surplus, I will not let it go, but will rather garner it like the dog, and in so doing will do my best to provide for myself in time of need, God willing.

For truly I do have need, insofar as I have been observed first by you, as was said above about the nature of THE WOLF, which shows me that I should be as wise as the dog in the story.

I remember further that the wolf has another nature which clearly shows me I must be on my guard. For I understand that it is so rigid that it cannot bend unless it swivels its whole body round. Wherefore I say, lord master, that I should be very foolish now if, without another word, I granted your request when I have neither the heart nor the will to make me do it, in conformity with the nature of THE VIPER.

For I understand that it attacks the clothed man and has no assurrance against the naked man. Do you think I am bound to attack you because you say you are clothed by your love for me? I have not clothed you with my love, rather you are quite naked of it. Therefore I fear you, which is not very surprising, in conformity with the nature of THE MONKEY. For you have told me that the monkey tries to imitate what it sees. In God's name this can help me. For after I saw you or another had spread nets to capture me, I should be crazy to come near. It is good to be barefooted and I would not believe anyone so foolish as to do what you say the monkey does after knowing this adventure.

By this argument which I see, lord and master, I tell you that you have spread your nets to capture me, and it behooves me to act in conformity with the nature of THE CROW. The crow is of such a nature that before its babies have black plumage like its own, it will not feed them. Likewise, I can tell you that because I would be contrary to your disposition and you to mine, and we would be in conflict both in habit and in will, I could not concur with your will, however much you might concur with mine.

You say further that the crow has a second nature by which I am bound to be improved. It seems to me that inasmuch as you say that the crow seizes man through his eyes and through them it extracts his brain, this is in contradiction with your words. For although Love captures man and woman through the eyes, it does not follow from that that the crow resembles Love. I say, rather, that one must with the eyes of the heart compare it to Hate. For inasmuch as man gets most help from the members that serve him, and this is taken from him first, one must consider that as Hate. And because I understand from you, lord and master, that the intelligence of man and woman resides in the brain and the crow robs him of that through his vision, I say that this is a sign of hatred, and I cannot compare it with Love, but with Treachery.

And so I say that I shall pay attention to the first nature of the crow: before I know that you agree with me I shall never agree to your request, for the nature of THE LION is not in agreement with this, as you yourself have taught me. I understand that when the lion eats its prey and man passes by it, the lion will attack the man if the man looks at it. Wherefore I say with conviction that I will not look at what might hurt me or at what might not be profitable to me. Rather I shall go where I know my advantage lies, to mold and perfect, if I can, what has not been well said or well conceived, as even THE LION does. The lion, as I understand from you, ejects a piece of flesh when giving birth, and that piece of flesh does not seem in the lion's judgment to be properly molded in its image. So the lion goes around it, shaping it with its tongue to its proper form. I long to do the same, lord master. If it happens that I must say something which I have not properly conceived, that is, thought out, I should like to go around it, molding it to sense and reason through the good doctrine which is available to me in your words.

Thus I am mindful of what I heard about THE WEASEL, namely that it conceives through its ear and gives birth through its mouth. I am truly anxious to remember this nature of the weasel. Conceiving through the ear and giving birth through the mouth has great significance. For I say that conception is something which involves great fear of initiating what will cause grievous suffering when one gives it birth. Ah, Lord God! Some people should be more careful than they are! For through them some will conceive a thing they hear, and to give it birth is so terrible and so dangerous! Some people throw out a word which they should have carried themselves until their dying day. For truly man and woman can do no worse than to give birth to, that is, utter, something unfitting which may destroy a kingdom.

God, I am so fearful of this that I do not know how to counsel myself. For if I uttered something I had conceived by ear and gave birth to it by mouth, I am very much afraid it would be venomous and would need to die, as is said of the weasel's babies. For when they are taken away from her, killed, and restored to the burrow, the mother knows by nature how to resuscitate them. But I am sure I could not do this, I have not learned how. Thus I must be on my guard much more than if I had the wisdom of THE CALADRIUS of which I have heard you tell.

For it is of such a nature that it knows when a sick man must get well or die, so that I have understood from you that when the bird is brought before a person who is lying sick in bed, it will turn its face away if he must die, but wondrously it looks him straight in the face if he will live. Wherefore I say that if I were as wise as the caladrius, I should not be wary of this act of giving birth, whatever the nature of the conception.

Oh God, protect me from conceiving anything that would be dangerous to bring to birth. And I shall not fail to protect myself also, provided that I am not as foolish as the man who falls asleep at the sweet song of The Siren. For it could certainly happen that I trusted myself to your fair words and sweet deceit, lord master, until soon I perished. So I must pay attention to The Asp, with which you made me wise. For, as you say, it guards the balm that drips down from the tree, and it cannot be tricked by any instrument's power because its ear is always watching against being lulled to sleep and losing sight of what it wants to guard.

In God's name, that serpent has strategy, subtlety, and subterfuge! So I certainly must pay it heed, then I shall not be deceived like The Tiger by the mirrors. For I clearly see and know that just as mirrors are strewn in front of the tiger to transfix it, so you produce for me your beautiful words. They are more delectable to hear than the tiger is to see, as has been said above, and I know well that you would not care who perished by them as long as your will be done.

Verily, master, if I were a woman to be transfixed like that, I should certainly need the true Panther. For it seems to me that I could not be drawn toward you in any way at all without being wounded. And I should be very fearful lest the panther might not be friendly to me. The panther is of such a nature that when some hurt or sick beast comes to it, the true panther will cure it with its sweet breath.

By God, here is sovereign medicine, and such a beast well deserves to be loved. For I know of a truth that there is no beast to be feared like the soft word that comes deceiving. And I truly believe that against that soft word one can have little protection, any more than one can against The Unicorn. By my faith, I fear that unicorn very much. For I know well that there is nothing so wounding as fair speech for, to tell the truth, nothing can pierce a hard heart like a soft and well-placed word.

And so, fair lord master, it would serve me well to be as wary as The Crane of which I heard you speak. For your words have hands and feet, and it truly seems that I can have no reason to deny you anything that you want. And yet the crane teaches me that I must not put any of my trust even in the most trustworthy thing in the world, any more than the crane that flies through the air. For when it rests on the ground it puts little pebbles inside one of its feet (because it is standing upon the other). And when it sleeps, the stones begin to fall, and the crane then rearranges itself to keep better vigil so that it cannot be surprised.

Certainly animals that possess such noble intelligence that they provide themselves with what can be painful to them are highly to be respected. Fair, sweet God, how one must respect the man or woman who knows how to provide against obvious misfortune and, even more, against misfortune in the dim and distant future! This is clearly signified for us in THE PEACOCK'S TAIL, as I heard previously. For it is true that a tail, insofar as it is to come (that is to say, is behind), signifies the obvious fact that those who travel along their way are not completely secure from evil men. And the person who wants to guard against them should not travel alone, but should travel with every provision to avoid surprise. The provident person is not quickly deceived.

Oh God, what is this providence? In God's name, that peacock's tail, which has so many eyes that it is bound to look ahead in more than one way demonstrates providence well to me, the more sorts of eyes are signified and shown us on the tail. For it seems to me that if one wishes to provide for oneself, it is necessary to see above, below, beside, and across. And I agree without reservation to this: that it is reasonable that if anyone does *not* wish to be on his guard like the crane mentioned above, he should suffer for it.

Oh God, how to be on guard? In God's name, THE LION now certainly shows me that. For I have heard that when it is chased by many people or by some other thing that may harm it, it covers and undoes its tracks with its tail. In this way it is not noticeable that anything has been there. Fair, sweet God, what a noble creature is this, which can do all this by its intelligence! In faith, it seems to me that if by chance I were induced through some defect of mine or through the faculty of speech to say or do something unreasonable, then I should pay attention to the peacock's tail and look at the direction from which I could most easily be harmed or helped. And if harm or misfortune should threaten, I should like to do like the lion, which covers with its tail what will possibly do it harm.

And so if I did something that was not good but, before I was damaged by it, I could right it before anyone perceived it, that should be considered as good sense on my part. For to wait until recovery is impossible is to repent too late. A woman would lose a great deal, even if she had as many eyes as has the peacock's tail and saw as clearly with each eye as if with one hundred but was then neglectful, as I heard concerning ARGUS. You told me he had a hundred eyes, and despite all that he was tricked and killed, as was said above.

And I believe without a doubt that if this Argus had been as wise as THE SWALLOW, which is of such a nature that it restores vision to its babies when someone has robbed them of it, he would still have been killed according as he was careless. For it is very clear, because he saw Mercurius was putting his eyes to sleep two by two, that Mercurius would put him to sleep in all his hundred eyes.

Thus for this reason sight is no use without something else. In the name of God, that is true. But what? In faith, I do not know, unless it be carefulness,* that is taking care to use what can serve in time of need. God, what is this need? In the name of God, the need to protect oneself from death—that is, not to lose one's honor. For the person who loses honor is indeed dead. Certainly that is true. And the person who is dead has little hope of recovery. For not everyone has THE WEASEL or THE PELICAN as a parent. For, as I heard before, those two have a nature to resuscitate their young. And thus it seems to me that it would not be good to put one's trust in Sight, if one is careless in another respect.

Fair, sweet God, how excellent a thing is total providence, and how much one must do to be completely provident! For there is no living creature, however wise and provident, that can be secure from the misfortunes that hold so much terror. For I understand that when it happens that a person has done something to the best of his ability and has no thought of fearing anyone, some malefactor will come to disturb him, throwing him into deep distress before he is finally restored to quiet, as I heard concerning THE WOODPECKER, which builds its nest in the tree's hollow where no other bird can enter. Then some fool comes to disturb it and stops up its nest. The woodpecker, unwilling to lose what it has built, seeks out a herb which by its nature it knows, applies the herb to the plug, and the plug jumps out.

If this bird is not to be valued highly—since by its intelligence it can recognize that herb—and if, moreover, I did not value the wise person who can save himself when something untoward happens, may I be damned, lord master!

Also I have heard you say there is a type of person that possesses the nature of THE SWALLOW. For you say that whatever the swallow does is done in flight. And by God, it is verily true that there are many people of this nature. When they engage themselves in one place, they do it in such a way as never really to approach, and they want to know everything, learn everything, but one can never learn anything from them. If anyone asks them something, they will never speak the truth about it but will say the opposite. And they will vary to and fro, one hour backward, the next hour forward. Thus, when one thinks to have pinned them down to some truth, it is fable, and they are quickly into some other point of view.

In God's name, lord and master, I have seen people like this, and one does well to beware of them if possible. For they take what belongs to another, and they cannot by another be taken any more than the swallow, which cannot be captured by any bird of prey unless by surprise. But there is nothing that cannot be captured by someone who is willing to take trouble and use guile. You have told me also about THE HEDGE-HOG, which is so spiny that it sticks out in all directions, but it can be captured only by spines. By God, that is certainly true, and I know well that there are many such people who cannot be caught unless by spines. But they are caught and held somehow, nevertheless, And I would like the men and women who hold such people to hold them so relentlessly that their needles and spines pierce their own bodies and they die for good and all.

And I believe with no hesitation that a man may be full of gentle words who would be very harsh and cutting if he had what he seeks, just like THE CAT, which at one moment has the sweetest face and softest, smoothest fur on the outside. But pull its tail, then it will show its claws on all four feet and tear your hands to shreds unless you quickly let it go. By God, I believe that a man also may for the moment behave very gently and say words to win confidence and to get his way, and yet he would do far worse than the cat can do, if he were on top and were not given all he wanted. It would be good to look out for such men.

And certainly, according as the swallow and the hedgehog cannot protect themselves at all times from being caught by some means, I am very fearful lest I be caught, whatever precautions I may have taken. For I very much fear that COCKATRICE of which I heard you speak. Fair lord master, although you say that when it has taken and devoured the man it wants, thereafterward it cries and grieves for him, that cannot do much good to the devoured or dead! For truly there is little hope of rescue after death. Wherefore I say that I am bound to fear that cockatrice very much. For if I were deceived by a man who had his way with me so that I lost my honor, anyone's lamenting would be of little use to me. For I know that I would then be held in poor esteem, and I know truly that who reverences and esteems me greatly now would then make fun of me. And then my heart would depart from me and I should die even more than that same cockatrice which THE HYDRA deceives, as you have told me. For it is true that the person in despair is much easier to deceive than the person who has all his wits about him. And because of what I have heard from you, I know truly that if I had anything by which I might be subjugated and some man who had designs on me were to come and deceive me until he got what he wanted with me, he then would afterward hold me in such disregard as I can now know well.

Oh fair, sweet God, keep me from this cockatrice, for upon my soul I have such fear of it that I shall never feel safe. For in God's name I am not of the nature of THE HYDRA, concerning which I have heard that when its head is cut off, two grow in its place. Certainly this could not happen to me. If anyone took away my honor, he would never bring it back to me. Rather I would have to do what I have heard THE SERRA does. For I believe that it follows the ship that is traveling over the high seas, and it wants to test itself at what in the end it cannot manage. Similarly, I know truly that if I were taken, as many are, I would have to act as if nothing degrading had happened to me. I would want to cover myself, and the less visible I was the more I would try to build my credibility and to malign, to cover my wrongdoing, those women who had suffered this misfortune. Verily! But in the end the truth would out. I would have to put down my false wings, which could not in the long run withstand the truth any more than the wind can force back the ship from moving ever forward while the water lasts. In God's name, the man who wants to do this thing I tell of *cannot do it*. People's pride and real life, good or evil, must be understood. Wherefore I say that if I could not hide my folly and my foolish enterprise, I should be as confused as THE SERRA, which plunges to the bottom of the sea.

Alas for me! What would then become of me? In God's name, I could then truly say that I would have to act like the miserable TURTLEDOVE when she has lost her mate, and refuses ever to take another. She will never again come to rest on verdure. And by God, in this same way I truly know that if such misfortune had befallen me, I would never again have happiness in me, and nobody would care. Moreover, if I were to strive for it, someone would say: "Look how that foolish woman would sell herself if she could find a buyer!"

Help me, God, help me! How could I ever be that sort of woman I am talking about? By the Holy Cross, if God please, it will not happen to me. I shall be wise and guard against error. Wherefore I shall not be as lazy as THE PARTRIDGE, for when she has laid, another partridge comes and takes her eggs and hatches them. But that is through some defect that is in her. She cannot endure the bother of hatching, or she thinks she cannot lose the babies because partridges return to their true mother. But even if it were not for either of these two reasons, yet I know truly that there can be no good justification for her not to hatch them, because she will never love them as much as if she had hatched them herself.

So also I can say concerning myself that if I do not strive to keep myself in check and to curb certain dispositions and desires that are not good, my eggs, that is the good words which I have heard from the natures of certain animals teaching me to guard what I have to guard, could certainly be stolen from me. Complaining would never serve me then, for there would be no recovery, although the partridge has one.

And certainly the partridge is not as foolish as I understand THE OSTRICH to be. For there is nothing in the ostrich to deserve that good news ever be heard about it. I have heard that when the ostrich has laid its egg, it will never look at it again. If that is not villainy on the ostrich's part and if it is not courtesy on the sun's part to rescue the egg by its warmth and hatch it so that the ostrich has no fear of losing it, may I be damned!

Ah lord master, how strongly I believe that if I put my trust in you as does the ostrich in the sun, you would rear me abominably! Cursed be anyone who trusts in you, however sincerely you behave. And I am not very courteous when I am not yet in your debt at all and yet have said so much. For it seems to me that there are few things as foolish as foolish speaking. According as I have heard concerning THE SCREECH OWL that when she has reared her baby birds until they are grown and she is so old that she can no longer fly, her babies pluck out all the feathers from her wings, for she would never moult by herself as other birds do, and they nourish her in their turn as much or more than she did them, God, could it be true at all, lord master, if I acted thus with you that you might do the same for me if there were need? Yes, you have told me so. But by the faith I owe God I am not yet reduced to the point where I feel bound to do this, and I do not know if ever I will do it, for it would be foolishness to swear something which one may have to abjure.

For I remain terribly fearful of something which, it seems to me, few people are without, namely pride, which you have compared to the beak of THE EAGLE. Certainly I say of a truth that pride is good as long as through pride one guards what should be guarded. For many people attribute to pride what honesty attributes to human nature, and this is clearly signified to us on various occasions. For I say truly that if I see someone who keeps me company and pretends to be charming for something he wants to get from me, or if it seems that by keeping company with me he will attain such improvement as he wishes to attain, reason shows me that I would not be improved thereby, but rather, damaged if I did not interpose a tower of cruelty, which some call pride. That is doubtless why I do not claim to have pride in excess of what is good for me, according to what I have understood from you. And I do not know, in conformity with the nature of THE CROCODILE which moves its upper jaw when eating, that this is unreasonable. It is *not*, for such is its nature.

So I can certainly say that if it happened that I actually loved anybody, in conformity with the nature of THE WOLF, I should then say that most passionately to the man who wanted to come close to me, if there were need, but I should do so only where I could not be captured, in conformity with the nature of THE MONKEY. For I well know that if I had something about which I did not want the world to be informed, it would be very much to my advantage to speak of it at my own discretion. Then I think that, although not concealed, yet it cannot do me as much harm as it can do me good. So that is not, I say, speech misused. But it would be speech misused if I were to say something which the man might want to use against me so that he would lord it over me. True love makes its presence clearly felt so that words and revelations between lovers, woman to man and man to woman, are nothing but speech misused. I do not say that a woman should not say to her lover, "I am happy that all the honor and good you can attain will be in my name," and that he for his part should not say to her, "Madame, (or Mademoiselle), I am in all sincerity at your disposition." But to say, "Lover, I am grieving (or dying) for you. If you do not rescue me, I am betrayed and shall die," those words are, in my view, "eating in the wrong way." I will never, by God, have any trust in him after he reveals himself in that way.

Nor would I have any confidence in such a lover but, in conformity with the nature of THE SHOD MONKEY, I would have greater trust in the man who had no ability to say what he wanted. For it truly seems to me that the man who puts on such a tragic act with words belongs to the category one can rightly call THE DRAGONS—they know how to flail around with their tongues so that they deceive poor, foolish women and with their flailing subjugate them. Ah true God, what great malice this is, how much this dragon is to be feared, and how I wish that no one would trust it until it were brought to the very fate they mention. In God's name, I wish women could be as prudent as I understand the female ELEPHANT to be. For I have clearly understood that she is very fearful of that dragon so that when she is about to give birth, she will place herself in a large stretch of water where there is an islet, and she will give birth there because of her fear of that dragon. For I understand the dragon's nature is so ardent that it cannot endure a lot of water any more than fire can. So because the female elephant fears the dragon, she places herself in the water, and she is still not secure if the male is not on the bank to stop the dragon if it were to come and try to enter the water.

I would truly like all women to guard themselves as does the female elephant so that when a man comes and acts despairingly, he would then be told something which he would do with the utmost reluctance, and from which least harm would ensue. And then after he did that, one would act thus as needed. But this is not the way things are, and there are women who believe whatever they hear, and who remain silent about what they see.

By my faith, THE DOVE then also signifies this clearly to us, according to what I have understood. For it seems to me that in all the world this is the bird that has the greatest fear of being captured. Wherefore I say that, as I have understood, it is wondrously wise and subtle. For because it fears to be captured or tricked, I believe it sits very willingly on water for the reason that water has the nature of a mirror, and the dove can see by the nature of the water if anything, even a bird of prey, whether falcon or sparrow hawk, wishes to harm it. Thus it sees from a distance their reflection in the water and because of this it flees for cover.

Wherefore there is nothing in this world as valuable as foresight, and water, which can give us such warning, is a truly marvelous thing. The dove teaches us to settle on water if we fear anything. Similarly, the elephant, which fears that diabolical dragon. And upon my soul both animals are absolutely right, for those two things are much to be feared. First, the dragon for its tongue that is envenomed to kill all the animals it touches with it.

Ah master, have we any such dragons among us? I truly believe and know we have, and I know well that they are worse than the feared dragon. And I shall tell you who they are and in what way they are worse, as I spoke above about those who act lovelorn till they die of it. *They* are calamitous. But I say upon my soul that a man may say he is dying of love when he does not even know of it as I, who by the grace of God am free of it, know love. And I say assuredly that these men are worse than the dragon mentioned above. For the dragon poisons only what it touches, but this false liar with his filthy, venomous old tongue spreads what he hopes will get him his way with the woman he covets, no matter how she may be damaged by him. Is there worse? Yes, indeed! If there were no worse, all would be well. But the evil dragon, the traitor, the wretch, now boasts that he has had his way. Is that an evil dragon? Certainly I say that no mortal man could take too cruel a vengeance on that dragon. What then will come of all this bragging? Can anyone else be hurt besides this poor, miserable, deceived woman?

In the name of God, yes. For I say that after he has flaunted himself, the woman comes despairing and she says by her good faith that she will not be the only woman deceived. Rather, she will come to another woman and will help to deceive her, that woman will do the same for a third, the third a fourth, the fourth a fifth, and so on. In the end, there are few women who have not been deceived, one through another. This is clearly signified to us by the hunters of wild birds. For I see that when they have lured one bird, they make that bird their decoy, and the other birds come to that bird and are led to capture. And all this happens principally through that diabolical dragon, which causes such women to be led astray.

The second thing that is much to be feared is that diabolical bird of prey that arrives so suddenly that there is scarcely anyone whom it does not surprise. I speak of those clerics who are so decked out with courtesy and fine words that there is no woman or maiden who can withstand them, whom they do not wish to take. And certainly I am in sympathy, for these men have every courtesy, as I have heard. Furthermore, it is from the handsomest men that clerics are made, and from the most devious in malice. They take the ignorant by surprise. Wherefore I call them birds of prey, and it would be good to have protection against them.

Oh God, how could one find a source of protection against their malice as the dove protects itself with a source of succor? In God's name, one could pay attention to THE ASP which guards the balm. I still see nothing that can be more useful. For anyone who listens to the clerics must conceive by ear, like the weasel which has been mentioned above. But this conception is worse than any other, because from it one does not give birth by mouth, but one must eventually die of it, like the dragon mentioned above. Anyone wanting to act like this could have as much confidence in clerics as can be had in THE WHALE.

The whale is a very large fish, and I certainly believe that those who cross the sea could think it an islet. Those who are tired and weary have an immense desire for rest and cool, and when they see this whale, they then believe the impossible, they disembark, and think they can do something that proves disagreeable to the whale. So the whale plunges to the bottom of the sea, thus drowning all who had trusted to it. And the whale itself is killed, for before it is wounded it stays motionless, but then the saltwater enters its flesh, causing it to come to shore where it is captured by this circumstance.

I can say the same of those women who believe of certain clerics who are simple in their manner that they are seemingly worthy of complete trust, so the women hang on their words and delight in them until one and the other are caught and completely undone. For the cleric loses a prebend from our Holy Church where he could be canon or bishop, and the maiden could have had a knightly gentleman who would give her more happiness and honor than the cleric, who has no comparable wealth.

Now, fair master, would you advise me to have any confidence in that Falcon, which swoops down so fast upon its prey from half a league above that the moment of its descent is impossible to determine, as it strikes death into its unsuspecting victim? Ah, Reynard, how far out your tongue is hanging! For no reason, of course, I suppose. I am sure that if Reynard were not hungry, his tongue would never hang out in the way I heard.

By God, master, I also believe that you would not have said the words I heard for no reason. Your hunger had to be appeased, whether by me or another woman. But it is the height of malice to feign sickness or death merely because one trembles. And it is surely not believable that this is anything else but trembling.

I am mindful of The Vulture which, I have heard, detects a carcass

that is a day's journey distant, although he feels no hunger. So I believe that you have the same nature as the vulture. For you have dealings with so many people and they with you, that you have heard someone speak of me in conversation, because I have a taste for conversation and cultured people. That is why, I believe, you came here first to find out who I was, and whether anything about me pleased you.

And I do not think, as I said at the beginning, that it was by courtesy that God did not wish to make us of inferior substance to men, rather He made us of man himself because He wishes us to be loved by men, and them in turn to be served by us. Wherefore, master, I truly believe that you see some grace in me so that it pleases you to say what I have heard. And the reason that I think you have spoken thus is none other than that you want me to protect myself from evil men. And because I have heard from you that one cannot know who is good and who is evil, it is expedient to guard against all men. And this I shall do until, through reason, mercy shall find its place. In my view, when a person does not wish to do a thing, there are multiple refusals. Let that suffice for good understanding.

Here ends the Response to Master Richard's Bestiary.

NOTES

Page 24

*A detailed description of this game is found in one of the variants transcribed by Segre at the base of p. 65. See also *Eine mittelneiderfränkische Ubertragung des Bestiaire d'Amour*, ed. J. Holmberg, p. 210, line 13.

Page 49

*I believe that the punctuation of M. Segre's text ("Par foi, je ne sai; se che n'est curieusités," p. 121) needs revision. Note that the primary meaning of "curiosité" in the thirteenth century ("care" or "carefulness") reflects more of the original "cura" than of the rare "curiositas."

BIBLIOGRAPHY

Ahrens, K. *Zur Geschichte des sogenannten Physiologus*. Ploen, 1885.

Ambrose, Saint. *Hexaemeron*. Ed. C. Schenkl, *Corpus Scriptorum Ecclesiasticorum*. Vol. XXXII, part I. Vienna, 1937.

Angremy, A. "Les oeuvres poétiques de Pierre de Beauvais," *Position des thèses de l'Ecole des Chartes* (1962), 17–21.

Auber, C. A., ed. and trans. *Physiologus Theobaldi*. Paris, 1884.

Bestiaire d'amour rimé, le. Ed. A. Thordstein. Lund-Copenhagen, 1941.

Biancotto, G., ed. and trans. *Bestiaires du moyen âge*. Paris, 1980.

Birkenmajer, A. "Robert Grosseteste and Richard de Fournival," *Medievalia et Humanistica* V (1948):36–41.

———. "Pierre de Limoges commentateur de Richard de Fournival," *Isis* XL (1949):18–31.

———. "La bibliothèque de Richard de Fournival, poète et érudit français du début du XIIIe siècle et son sort ultérieur," *Etudes d'histoire des sciences et de la philosophie du moyen âge, Studia copernica* I (1970):117–215.

Bormans, M. "Notice sur deux fragments manuscrits de poésies thyoises de la fin du XIIIe siècle (*le Bestiaire d'amours* et *l'Art d'aimer* d'Ovide)," *Bulletin de l'Académie Royale des sciences, des lettres et des beaux-arts de Belgique* II, 27 (1864):488–506.

Cahier, C., and A. Martin. *Mélanges d'archéologie, d'histoire et de littérature* I–IV. Paris, 1847–1856.

Cahier, C. *Nouveaux mélanges*. 4 vols. Paris, 1874–1877.

Calonne, Baron Albéric de. *Histoire de la ville d'Amiens*. 2 vols. Amiens, 1899–1900.

Carlill, J. *Physiologus*. London, 1824.

Carmody, F. J., ed. *Physiologus Latinus, éditions préliminaires, Versio B*. Paris, 1939.

———. *Physiologus Latinus, Versio Y*. University of California Publications in Classical Philology XII (1933–1944):95–134.

———. *Physiologus, The Very Ancient Book of Beasts, Plants, and Stones*. San Francisco, 1953.

———. "*De bestiis et aliis rebus* and the Latin *Physiologus*," *Speculum* XIII (1938):153–159.

Cocheris, H. *La Vieille ou les Dernières Amours d'Ovide*. Paris, 1861.

Cohn, C. *Geschichte des Einhorns*. Berlin, 1896.

Crespo, R. *Una versione pisana inedita del "Bestiaire d'Amours."* Leiden, 1972.

Cronin, G. "The Bestiary and the Mediaeval Mind—Some Complexities," *Modern Language Quarterly* II (1941):191–198.

Dalton, O. M. *Early Christian Art, a Survey of Monuments*. Oxford, 1925.

De Champeaux, G., and S. Sterckx. *Introduction au monde des symboles*. St.-Léger Vauban, 1966.

Delisle, Léopold, L. "*La Biblionomie* de Richard de Fournival," *Cabinet des manuscrits de la Bibliothèque Nationale II*. Paris, 1874, 518–535.

Denifle, H., and E. Chatelain. *Chartularium Universitatis Parisiensis*. 4 vols. Paris, 1889–1897.

Denis, F. *Le monde enchanté, cosmographie et histoire naturelle fantastiques du moyen âge*. Paris, 1843.

Deschamps, N., and R. Bruno. "L'univers des bestiaires. Dossier bibliographique et choix de textes," *Etudes françaises* X, 3 (August 1974): 231–282.

De Solons, E., and Dom C. Jean-Nesmy. *Bestiaire roman*. St. Léger Vauban, 1977.

Dicta Chrysostomi, Münchener Texte, Heft 8 B (Kommentar), 1916, 13–52.

Druce, G. C. *The Bestiary of Guillaume le Clerc*. Translated into English. Printed for private circulation. Kent, 1936.

———. "The Elephant in Medieval Legend and Art," *The Journal of the British Archaeological Association* LXXVI (1919):1–73.

———. "Legend of the Serra or Saw-Fish," *Proceedings of Society of Antiquaries of London*, 2d series, XXXI (1919):20–35.

———. "The Medieval Bestiaries, and their Influence on Ecclesiastical Decorative Art," *The Journal of the British Archaeological Association*, new series, XXV (1919):41–82; XXVI (1920):35–79.

Druce, G. C. "The Symbolism of the Crocodile in the Middle Ages," *The Journal of the British Archaeological Association* LXVI (1909):311–338.

Du Cange, C. *Extraits du Chartulaire du Chapitre de Notre-Dame d'Amiens*. MSS Du Cange. (BN. fr. 9497).

———. *Histoire des évêques d'Amiens*. MSS Du Cange. (BN. fr. 9476).

Duncan, T. S. "The Weasel in Religion, Myth, and Superstition," *Washington University Studies* (Humanistic Series) XII (1924):33–66.

Epiphanius. *Physiologus*, ed. J. P. Migne, *Patrologia Graeca* XLIII, cols. 518–534.

Faral, E. "La queue de poisson des sirènes," *Romania* LXXIV (1953):433–506.

Garver, M. S. "Sources of the Beast Similes in the Italian Lyric of the Thirteenth Century," *Romanische Forschungen* XXI (1905–1908):276–320.

———. *Supplementary Italian Bestiary Chapters, Romanic Review* XI (1920): 308–327.

Gervaise. *Le bestiaire de Gervaise*. Ed. P. Meyer. *Romania* I (1872):420–443.

Ginzberg, L. *Legends of the Jews*. Trans. H. Szold. Philadelphia, 1909.

Glorieux, P. "Etudes sur la 'Biblionomia' de Richard de Fournival," *Recherches de théologie ancienne et médiévale* XXX (1963):205–231.

Glorieux, P. "La bibliothèque de Gérard d'Abbeville," *Recherches de théologie ancienne et médiévale* XXXVI (1969):48–83.

———. "Aux origines de la Sorbonne, I: Robert de Sorbon," *Etudes de philosophie médiévale* LIII, 82–83; 239–289.

Goldstaub, M. "Der *Physiologus* und seine Weiterbildung," *Philologus, Supplementband* VII (1899–1901):339–414.

Grundriss der romanischen Literaturen des Mittelalters. Vol. VI: *La littérature didactique, allégorique et satirique* I (1968); II (1970).

Guillaume le Clerc. *Le bestiaire.* Ed. C. Hippeau. Caen, 1852; repr. Geneva, 1970.

———. *Le bestiaire. Das Thierbuch des Normanischen Dichters Guillaume le Clerc.* Ed. R. Reinsch. Leipzig, 1892.

Halliday, W. R. "Picus-Who-Is-Also-Zeus," *Classical Review* XXXVI (1922): 110–112.

Ham, E. B., ed. "The Cambrai Bestiary," *Modern Philology* XXXVI (1939): 225–237.

Heider, G. "*Physiologus* nach einer Handschrift des XI. Jahrhunderts," *Archiv für die Kunde österreichischer Geschichts-Quellen* V (1850):541–582.

Holmberg, J. *Eine mittelniederfränkische Übertragung des "Bestiaire d'amour," sprachlich untersucht und mit altfranzösischen Paralleltext.* Uppsala, 1925.

Hulme, E. F. *Natural History Lore and Legend.* London, 1895.

Isidore of Seville. *Etymologiarum sive originum, libri XX.* Ed. W. M. Lindsay. Oxford, 1911.

James, M. R. *The Bestiary.* Oxford, 1928.

Janson, H. W. *Apes and Ape Lore in the Middle Ages and the Renaissance.* London, 1952.

Jauss, H. R. *Genèse de la poésie allégorique française au moyen âge (de 1180 à 1240).* Heidelberg, 1962.

———. "Rezeption und Poetiserung des *Physiologus*," *Grundriss der romanischen Literaturen des Mittelalters* VI/1. Heidelberg, 1968.

Kaikamis, D., ed., *Der Physiologus nach der ersten Redaktion.* Meisenheim am Glan, 1974.

Keller, O. *Die antike Tierwelt,* 2 vols. Leipzig, 1909.

Klopsch, P. *Pseudo-Ovidius De Vetula. Untersuchungen und Text.* Leiden-Köln, 1967.

Krappe, A. "The Historical Background of Philippe de Thaun's *Bestiaire*," *Modern Language Notes* LIX (1944):325–327.

Künstle, K. *Ikonographie.des christlichen Kunst* I–II. Freiburg, 1928.

Långfors, A. "*L'Arrière-ban d'amours*, poème du xiiie siècle, inspiré par *le*

Bestiaire d'amours de Richard de Fournival," *Mélanges J. Melander*. Uppsala, 1943, 284–290.

———. "*Le Bestiaire d'amours en vers* par Richard de Fournival," *Mémoires de la Société néophilologique de Helsingfors* VII (1924):291–317.

Langlois, Ch.-V. *La connaissance de la nature et du monde*. Vol. III of *La vie en France au moyen âge*. 2d ed. Paris, 1927.

———. "Un document relatif à Richard de Fournival," *Mélanges d'archéologie et d'histoire* X (1890):123–125.

———. "Quelques oeuvres de Richard de Fournival," *Bibliothèque de l'Ecole des Chartes* LXV (1904):101–115.

Lauchert, F. *Geschichte des Physiologus*. Strassburg, 1889.

Lozinski, G. "Un fragment du *Bestiaire d'amour* de Richard de Fournival." *Romania* LI (1925):561–568.

Lum, P. *Fabulous Beasts*. London, 1952.

McCulloch, F. *Medieval Latin and French Bestiaries*. Chapel Hill, 1960.

———. "The Metamorphoses of the Asp," *Studies in Philology* LVI (1959): 7–14.

McLeod, W. M. "The *Consaus d'amours* of Richard de Fournival," *Studies in Philology* XXXII/1 (Jan. 1935):1–21.

Mai, A. "Excerpta ex *Physiologo*," *Classici Auctores* VII (1835):589–596.

Manitius, M. *Geschichte der lateinischen Literatur des Mittelalters* III, 731 ff. Munich, 1931.

Mann, M. F. "Der *Bestiaire divin* des Guillaume le Clerc," *Französische Studien* VI (1888):37–73.

———. "Der *Physiologus* des Philipp von Thaün und seine Quellen," *Anglia* VII (1884):420–468; IX (1886):391–434, 447–450.

Menhardt, H. "Der Millstätter *Physiologus* und seine Verwandten," *Kärntner Museumsschriften* XIV (1956).

Meyer, P. "Les Bestiaires," *Histoire littéraire de la France* XXXIV (1914):362–390.

Mioland, Mgr. J.-M. *Actes de l'Eglise d'Amiens*. Vol. I. Amiens, 1848.

Mozley, J. H. "Le *De Vetula*, poème pseudo-ovidien," *Latomus* II (1938):53–72.

Oxford Dictionary of the Christian Church, ed. F. L. Cross and E. A. Livingstone, 2d ed. London, 1974, 385.

Paris, P. "Notice sur la vie et les ouvrages de Richard de Fournival," *Bibliothéque de l'Ecole des Chartes* II (1840–1841):32–56.

———. "Richard de Fournival," *Histoire littéraire de la France* XXIII (1856): 708–733.

Perry, B. E. "*Physiologus*," *Real-Encyclopädie der classischen Altertumswissenschaft*, Neue Bearbeitung, XX (1950):1074–1129.

Peters, E. trans. *Der Physiologus*. Munich, 1921.

Petrus Comestor, *Historia Scholastica*. Ed. D. H. Vollmer. Berlin, 1925.

Philippe de Thaun. *Le Bestiaire*. Ed. E. Walberg. Paris, 1900; repr. Geneva, 1970.

Philippe de Thaun. *Le Bestiaire*. Ed. T. Wright. London, 1841.

Pickford, C. F. "The *Roman de la rose* and a Treatise attributed to Richard de Fournival: two manuscripts in the John Rylands Library," *Bulletin of the John Rylands Library* XXXIV (1952):333–365.

Pierre de Beauvais. *Bestiaire en prose de Pierre le Picard*. Ed. C. Cahier and A. Martin, *Mélanges d'archéologie, d'histoire et de littérature* II (1851):85–100, 106–232; III (1853):203–288; IV (1856):55–87.

———. *Le Bestiaire de Pierre de Beauvais*. Ed. G. Mermier. Paris, 1977.

Pitra, J. B., ed. *Physiologus: Fragments alphabétiques*. Paris, 1855.

Richard de Fournival. *Le Bestiaire d'amour*. Ed. C. Hippeau. Paris, 1860.

———. *Li Bestiaires d'Amours di Maistre Richart de Fornival e li Response du Bestiaire*. Ed. C. Segre. Milan-Naples, 1957.

———. *Biblionomia*. Ed. L. Delisle. *Cabinet des manuscrits de la Bibliothèque Nationale* II:518–535. Paris, 1874.

———. "La 'Biblionomia' de Richard de Fournival du manuscrit 636 de la Sorbonne, textes et facsimilé avec la transcription de L. Delisle." *Mousaion* LXII (1965).

———. *L'Oeuvre lyrique de Richard de Fournival*. Ed. Y. Lepage. Ottawa, 1981.

———. *Kritischer Text der Lieder Richards de Fournival*. Ed. P. Zarifopol. Halle, 1904.

Rigaud de Barbezieux. *Poésies*. Ed. C. Chabaneau and J. Anglade. Montpellier, 1919.

Robathan, D. M. "Introduction to the Pseudo-Ovidian *De Vetula*," *Transactions and Proceedings of the American Philological Association* LXXXVIII (1957):197–207.

———. *The Pseudo-Ovidian De Vetula*. Amsterdam, 1968.

Rouse, R. H. "The Early Library of the Sorbonne," *Scriptorium* XXI (1967): 42–71, 227–251.

———. "Manuscripts Belonging to Richard de Fournival," *Revue d'histoire des textes* III (1973):253–269.

———. "A Text of Seneca's Tragedies in the Thirteenth Century," *Revue d'histoire des textes* I (1971):93–121.

Saly, A. "*Li Commens d'amours* de Richard de Fournival (?)," *TraLiLi* X/2 (1972): 21–55.

Sbordone, F., ed. *Physiologus*. Milan, 1936.

———. *Ricerche sulle fonti e sulla compozione del Physiologus greco.* Naples, 1936.

Seel, O. *Der Physiologus, übertragen und erläutert.* Zurich, 1960.

Seidler, E. "Die Medizin in der 'Biblionomia' des Richard de Fournival," *Sudhoffs Archiv* LI (1967):44–54.

Shephard, O. *The Lore of the Unicorn.* London, 1930.

Speroni, G. B. "Il 'Consaus d'amours' di Richard de Fournival," *Medioevo romanzo* I/2 (1974):217–278.

———. *La Poissance d'amours dello pseudo-Richard de Fournival.* Florence, 1975.

Strzygowski, J. "Der Bilderkreis des griechischen *Physiologus*," *Byzantinisches Archiv* II (1899):1–130.

Theobaldi Physiologus. Ed. and trans. P. T. Eden. Leiden, 1972.

———. *Physiologus—a Metrical Bestiary of Twelve Chapters by Bishop Theobald.* Trans. A. W. Rendell. London, 1928.

Thibaut de Champagne. *Les Chansons de Thibaut de Champagne.* Ed. A. Wallensköld. Paris, 1925.

Thierfelder, J. G. "Eine Handschrift des *Physiologus Theobaldi*," *Serapeum* XV–XVI (1862):225–231, 241–243.

Thomas, J. "Un art d'aimer du XIIIe siècle: *L'amistiés de vraie amour*," *Revue belge de philologie et d'histoire* XXXVI (1958):786–811.

Thordstein, A., ed., *Le Bestiaire d'amour rimé, poème inédit du XIIIe siècle.* Lund-Copenhagen, 1941.

Thorndike, E. and P. Kibre. *A Catalogue of Incipits of Mediaeval Scientific Writings in Latin.* Cambridge, 1937.

———. *A History of Magic and Experimental Science.* 2 vols. New York, 1929.

Tobler, A. "Lateinische Beispielsammlung mit Bildern," *Zeitschrift für romanische Philologie* XII (1888):57–88.

Van Lantschoot, A. "A propos du *Physiologus*," reprinted from *Coptic Studies in Honor of Walter Ewing Crum. Byzantine Institute Bulletin* II (1950):339–363.

Vitte, S. "Richard de Fournival. Etudes sur sa vie et ses oeuvres, suivie de l'édition du *Bestiaire d'amour*, de la *Réponse de la dame* et des *Chansons*," *Positions des thèses de l'Ecole des Chartes* (1929):223–227.

Wellmann, M. "Der *Physiologus*, eine religionsgeschichtlich-naturwissenschaftliche Untersuchung," *Philologus*, Supplementband XXII, Heft I (1930):1–116.

White, L., jr. *The Book of Beasts.* New York, 1960.

———. "Natural Science and Naturalistic Art in the Middle Ages," *American Historical Review* LII (1947):421–435.

Woledge, B., and H. P. Clive. *Répertoire des plus anciens textes en prose française.* Geneva, 1964.

protection, xix, xx, xxiii, 6, 17, 34, 44, 46, 47, 48, 49, 56, 58
Provençal, xix
providence, 48, 49, 54
prowess, 25
publicity, 17, 25, 32, 33, 34, 51, 53
Puissance d'amours, xiv
pute escole, xxvi

quarrel, 26, 27, 45

rank, 31, 43
reading, 2
rear, 28, 52, 53
reason, xxii, xxiii, 21, 22, 36, 41, 42, 43, 46, 47, 48, 53, 58
recovery, 10, 20, 22, 46, 47, 49, 52
refusal, xxvi, 9, 20, 22, 45, 47, 58
religious terminology, xx
remedy, 18, 21, 22, 44, 47, 48, 52
repentance, xx, 19, 23, 48
repetition, xx
resemblance, 8
response, xxii–xxvi, 41
restraint, 52
resuscitate, 46, 49, 51
retain, 28, 29, 30, 33, 34
retainers, 2, 43
Reynard, xxvi, 57
rhetoric, xxi
rib, 42
Richard de Fournival, xiii–xxi
river, 33
Robert de Sommercote, xiii
Roger de Fournival, xiii
romance, 1, 2

Roman de la Rose, ix
Roman de Renart, ix
Rouen, xiii
rough, 12

sadness, 13, 52
St. Denis, 31
salamander, 13
sand, 30, 35
satire, ix
screech-owl, xviii, xix, 30, 31, 52, 53
Scripture, 42
sea, 26, 27, 31, 51, 56
secrecy, 25, 32
senses, xv, 12, 13, 14, 15, 16, 17
serpent, 23
serra, xviii, 26, 51
service, 15, 25, 30, 35, 36, 43, 54, 58
shame, 6, 8, 51
shatter, 31, 32
sheepfold, 6
ship, 26, 51
shoes, xix, 7
sickness, 10, 18, 19, 46, 47, 57
sight, xv, 1, 2, 8, 9, 12, 13, 14, 15, 16, 22, 34, 43, 44, 45, 47, 48, 49
similes, ix, xvi, xvii, xviii, xix, xx xxiii
sin, xxv, 42
siren, xviii, xxv, 10, 11, 16, 18, 47
skin, 12, 35
sleep, 10, 11, 14, 15, 16, 17, 18, 42, 47, 49
smell, 12, 13, 15, 16
smooth, 12

Master Richard's Bestiary of Love and Response
was set in Monotype Dante. Designed by Giovanni Mardersteig,
the type was cast by Michael & Winifred Bixler at their typefoundry
in Skaneateles, New York. The calligraphic versals are the work of
Yvette Rutledge. The original of this book is a
letterpress edition, which was designed by
Barry Moser & P. Chase Twichell, and issued by the
Pennyroyal Press, West Hatfield, Massachusetts.
The University of California edition was prepared under the
direction of Czeslaw Jan Grycz and printed at Malloy Lithographing
in Ann Arbor, Michigan, on 80 pound Glatfelter paper.
The Jacket and Binding were Designed by Steve Renick.